Intergovernmental Panel On Climate Change (IPCC) Third Assessment Report

United States Congress Senate Committee on Commerce, Science, and Transportation

This work has been selected by scholars as being culturally important, and is part of the knowledge base of civilization as we know it. This work was reproduced from the original artifact, and remains as true to the original work as possible. Therefore, you will see the original copyright references, library stamps (as most of these works have been housed in our most important libraries around the world), and other notations in the work.

This work is in the public domain in the United States of America, and possibly other nations. Within the United States, you may freely copy and distribute this work, as no entity (individual or corporate) has a copyright on the body of the work.

As a reproduction of a historical artifact, this work may contain missing or blurred pages, poor pictures, errant marks, etc. Scholars believe, and we concur, that this work is important enough to be preserved, reproduced, and made generally available to the public. We appreciate your support of the preservation process, and thank you for being an important part of keeping this knowledge alive and relevant.

S. Hrg. 107–1027
INTERGOVERNMENTAL PANEL ON CLIMATE CHANGE (IPCC) THIRD ASSESSMENT REPORT

HEARING
BEFORE THE

COMMITTEE ON COMMERCE, SCIENCE, AND TRANSPORTATION UNITED STATES SENATE

ONE HUNDRED SEVENTH CONGRESS

FIRST SESSION

MAY 1, 2001

Printed for the use of the Committee on Commerce, Science, and Transportation

U.S. GOVERNMENT PRINTING OFFICE
WASHINGTON : 2004

For sale by the Superintendent of Documents, U.S. Government Printing Office
Internet: bookstore.gpo.gov Phone: toll free (866) 512–1800; DC area (202) 512–1800
Fax: (202) 512–2250 Mail: Stop SSOP, Washington, DC 20402–0001

SENATE COMMITTEE ON COMMERCE, SCIENCE, AND TRANSPORTATION

ONE HUNDRED SEVENTH CONGRESS

FIRST SESSION

JOHN MCCAIN, Arizona, *Chairman*

TED STEVENS, Alaska
CONRAD BURNS, Montana
TRENT LOTT, Mississippi
KAY BAILEY HUTCHISON, Texas
OLYMPIA J. SNOWE, Maine
SAM BROWNBACK, Kansas
GORDON SMITH, Oregon
PETER G. FITZGERALD, Illinois
JOHN ENSIGN, Nevada
GEORGE ALLEN, Virginia

ERNEST F. HOLLINGS, South Carolina
DANIEL K. INOUYE, Hawaii
JOHN D. ROCKEFELLER IV, West Virginia
JOHN F. KERRY, Massachusetts
JOHN B. BREAUX, Louisiana
BYRON L. DORGAN, North Dakota
RON WYDEN, Oregon
MAX CLELAND, Georgia
BARBARA BOXER, California
JOHN EDWARDS, North Carolina
JEAN CARNAHAN, Missouri

MARK BUSE, *Republican Staff Director*
ANN CHOINIERE, *Republican General Counsel*
KEVIN D. KAYES, *Democratic Staff Director*
MOSES BOYD, *Democratic Chief Counsel*

CONTENTS

	Page
Hearing held on May 1, 2001	1
Statement of Senator McCain	1
Statement of Senator Stevens	7
Prepared statement of Senator Kerry	69

WITNESSES

Craig, Hon. Larry E., U.S. Senator from Idaho	2
Hagel, Hon. Chuck, U.S. Senator from Nebraska	4
Hansen, Dr. James, Director, Goddard Institute for Space Studies, National Aeronautics and Space Administration	42
Prepared statement	44
Lindzen, Dr. Richard S., Massachussetts Institute of Technology	24
Prepared statement	27
McCarthy, James J., Director, Museum of Comparative Zoology, Harvard University	19
Prepared statement	21
Ramaswamy, Dr. Venkatachala, Senior Scientist, Geophysical Fluids Dynamics Laboratory, National Oceanic and Atmospheric Administration	9
Prepared statement	11
Sathaye, Dr. Jayant A., Senior Scientist, Lawrence Berkeley National Laboratory, University of California	31
Prepared statement	33

APPENDIX

Response by Dr. Venkatachala Ramaswamy to written questions submitted by Hon. John McCain	70
Response by Dr. James J. McCarthy to written questions submitted by Hon. John McCain	75
Response by Dr. James Hansen to written questions submitted by Hon. John McCain	77
Response by Dr. Richard S. Lindzen to written questions submitted by:	
Hon. John McCain	84
Hon. John Kerry	85

INTERGOVERNMENTAL PANEL ON CLIMATE CHANGE (IPCC) THIRD ASSESSMENT REPORT

TUESDAY, MAY 1, 2001

U.S. SENATE,
COMMITTEE ON COMMERCE, SCIENCE, AND TRANSPORTATION,
Washington, DC.

The Committee met, pursuant to notice, at 9:30 a.m. in room SR–253, Russell Senate Office Building, Hon. John McCain, Chairman of the Committee, presiding.

OPENING STATEMENT OF HON. JOHN McCAIN, U.S. SENATOR FROM ARIZONA

The CHAIRMAN. Good morning. Last year, we held three hearings on the issue of climate change. Today we hope to continue the dialog on this very important matter confronting not only the nation but the world. In recent discussions surrounding the President's position on the Kyoto Protocol there were several questions concerning the availability of sound science in the decisionmaking process.

At this hearing, we hope to have an open and frank discussion on the recent third assessment report by the Intergovernmental Panel on Climate Change. The IPCC efforts are recognized as one of the most comprehensive in this matter. It involves the work of hundreds of scientists from around the world.

The third assessment report is an up-to-date assessment of published and peer-reviewed policy relevant scientific, technical, and socioeconomic literature. The previous assessment report was issued 5 years ago. The latest report concludes that a firmer association between human activities and climate seems to have emerged. I look forward to discussing the basis for such a conclusion by the panel.

I am disappointed, but not surprised to hear that the most vulnerable to these changing conditions are those with the least resources. The report states the effects of climate change are expected to be the greatest in developing countries in terms of loss of life and effects on investment and the economy. Therefore, the developed countries like the United States must do its share in addressing this global problem.

Any agreement on the Kyoto Protocol will have real effects on our economy. It is interesting to note that the report indicates that about half of the emissions reductions targets may be achieved with a net economic benefit, according to the report. This sounds like the basis for action to me.

While we appreciate the work of the hundreds of scientists involved in this effort, we recognize that a substantial amount of research remains before we can fully understand the complex and dynamic relationship between the atmosphere, the oceans, land, and mankind. I plan to review the U.S. research contributions to this global problem to ensure that our contributions are helpful and adequate.

I note that much of the assessment report is based upon computer models, and I must say that I am alarmed to hear about the recent National Research Council's report on the shortcomings of the U.S. climate modeling program. We hope that today's discussion will go a long way in aiding this Committee and the Congress in crafting future actions to address this issue. This is the fourth hearing we have held on this topic in the past year.

I plan to work with the other members of this Committee and the Senate, along with our witnesses today, to determine the appropriate next step in this complicated process of addressing the changing global climate. I welcome all of our witnesses here today. We would like to start with our two colleagues from the Senate, Senator Craig and Senator Hagel, and obviously we would appreciate your remarks and hope that they can be relatively brief.

Senator Craig, welcome.

STATEMENT OF HON. LARRY E. CRAIG, U.S. SENATOR FROM IDAHO

Senator CRAIG. Well, Mr. Chairman, certainly I thank you for convening this hearing today, and I think you and I both agree that the potential of climate change is a serious issue with high stakes. I do believe that premature government action to cut back energy use to levels lower than those in the growth-oriented nineties could cool the economy faster than it cools the climate.

On the other hand, you and I agree that ignoring the concerns expressed by some respected scientists about recent warming trends is equally irresponsible. During the last 4 years, Mr. Chairman, you have held hearings, I have held hearings, Senator Hagel, I, and a good many others have been involved in the fascinating issue.

I have traveled to Woods Hole to listen to the scientists. I have traveled to the Hague to see the international politics of this. I have attended numerous hearings. I have listened and read the testimony out of the hearings that you have assembled. Clearly, the scientific community has made impressive gains in its understanding of global climate change, but with increased understanding has come increased uncertainty about the relative roles of greenhouse gases, aerosols, land coverage changes, ocean currents, in the last century's temperature changes.

In my opinion, Mr. Chairman, moving ahead with strict government action based upon our current best guess of what we are thinking is not a wise action. This is especially true in light of the potential economic and national security implications that are likely as consequences of restricting our nation's energy use.

What is needed at this time, Mr. Chairman, is steady and thoughtful leadership, and I think your hearings demonstrate that national policy on this issue must evolve commensurately with the increasing confidence we achieve in our scientific understanding. Consensus on appropriate action should be the cornerstone of our national policy on this issue.

The National Academy of Science, upon the authority of a charter granted by the Congress in 1863, has a mandate that requires it to advise our government on scientific and technical matters. The creation of the United Nations Intergovernmental Panel on Climate Change, which you have referenced, the IPCC, does not, indeed, should not, extinguish the mandate of the National Academy to advise our government on scientific and technical matters.

Let me be clear, Mr. Chairman, that I am not here today to impugn the work of the scientists associated with the IPCC's third assessment. Frankly, after conferring with many of the scientists who are credentialed in the disciplines of atmospheric and ocean science, I am quite confident that much of the underlying work contained in the assessment is relatively sound. However, these same scientists who I have conferred with caution that the conclusions contained in the assessment summary, much of which have been reported by the media, are by no means certain and, at the very least, in need of scrutiny.

The computer modeling that you referenced in your opening statement, Mr. Chairman, is a part of our concern. In my opinion, the President of the National Academy of Science should be tasked to review the IPCC Third Assessment conclusions, for the following reasons:

First, The National Academy, through its operating arm, the National Research Council, has been reviewing the science of climate change for most of two decades.

Second, many of the scientists involved in the NRC research on climate change have contributed scientific analysis to the IPCC's third assessment.

And, finally, the NRC has prepared recent reports themselves, a synthesis of many other studies, that are useful guides to the state of knowledge and the requirements for the scientific path forward.

Mr. Chairman, I have reviewed the recent scientific reports, as I know you have. The NRC's "Pathways" and "Climate Modeling" reports raise some profoundly important questions. Our best policy decisions could turn on answers to any of them. Now, the "Pathways" report stated that presently available observation and modeling information—again, you have expressed that concern on climate change—is useful, but cannot provide the knowledge needed to make informed decisions on the kinds of critical policies that we would direct.

The most recent National Research Council's report, "The Science of Regional and Global Change—Putting Knowledge to Work," which I and Senator Hagel and Senator Murkowski made available to all Senators in March, reaffirms the very findings and the very concerns I am expressing. Last week, I met with Charles Kennel, who co-authored that report and has chaired a NRC Committee on climate change, also heads up the Scripps Institution of Oceanography out at La Jolla. He expressed those concerns, and suggests some approaches to bringing about a better modeling system.

In addition, Mr. Chairman, the National Academy recognizes the legitimacy of our concern about the increasing use of science as an advocacy tool for political agendas by making the following statement on page 10 of that report:

> "Research on how to do more effective, credible, and helpful scientific assessment is badly needed. Of particular importance will be the development of assessment processes, that link knowledge producers and users in a dialog that builds a mutual understanding of what is needed, what can credibly be said, and how it can be said in a way that maintains both scientific credibility, and political legitimacy."

The National Academy proposes solid recommendations for implementing an effective research agenda, and I strongly endorse them.

Mr. Chairman, the National Academy is putting together and inviting all of us to a high-level, half-day forum at the Academy's headquarters that I would encourage all of us to attend. I have encouraged Paul O'Neill of the Treasury to be an attendee. He is an outspoken person on this issue. Clearly, we need to consult with our scientists, but in the process, I do believe we need to build computer models that we can rely on, and not rely on international models that do not have the sensitivity to a variety of the concerns, but most importantly, to the quality of the science involved.

Well, you have urged us to be brief, and I will conclude. There are important issues to be dealt with here, Mr. Chairman Thorough vetting by this Committee and others is critical, but I do believe we have come a long way, but I do not believe that the science today or the modeling available that brings that science together will lead us to a basis for sound policymaking. I think it is our responsibility to bring all of those tools together.

In visiting with Dr. Kennel the other day, he made it clear our science is good. The problem is, Mr. Chairman, is that the science is over here, and the modeling capability is over there, and we have not put those two together yet. We have all of those resources in our government. We have the supercomputers at the Department of Energy, and we have the brain trust that has been assembled by the National Research Council through the National Academy of Science. I think it is our responsibility to not only drive the process that helps put the proper models together and brings the resources of our federal government together that will allow us, this Committee and other committees, the kind of sound decisionmaking based on good science that the policy for this country demands.

Thank you very much.

The CHAIRMAN. Thank you, Senator Craig.

Senator Hagel.

STATEMENT OF HON. CHUCK HAGEL, U.S. SENATOR FROM NEBRASKA

Senator HAGEL. Mr. Chairman, thank you. I, like our colleague, Senator Craig, am grateful for an opportunity to come before your Committee this morning and discuss an issue that I have been deeply involved in over the last several years. I have come across few issues, Mr. Chairman, more complex than climate change. What exactly is happening? What is the science? Are the actions of humans having a real impact on climate change? What is the future?

Most importantly, I think we asked ourselves, what do we do? None of these questions have simple answers We do know there has been climate change since the beginning of time. In fact, very radical climate change, long before the industrial revolution or the internal combustion engine.

Climate change, Mr. Chairman, is not new. In addressing this complicated issue, I start with this premise. Debate over climate change is not a question of who is for or against the environment. We all support protecting our involvement. I have yet to meet a Senator or any public official who wants to leave dirty air, dirty water, or a degraded environment as the legacy for his or her children. There may be one, Mr. Chairman. I have not met him or her.

Over the last 3 months, three scientific working groups of the Intergovernmental Panel on Climate Change, IPCC, have released thousands of pages of their work for the IPCC's assessment. The summaries of those reports are written not by the scientists, Mr. Chairman, but by U.N. environmental activists. There is a reason the organization is called the Intergovernmental Panel on Climate Change. The summaries are political documents drafted by government representatives after intense negotiating sessions. In some cases, the very people sent to represent their countries in writing the IPCC summaries are later working to negotiate the provisions of the Kyoto Protocol, so you have the same people defining the problems who are also trying to create a solution.

The working group reports vary widely in their scientific conclusions and predictions for global warming during the next century, but the summaries tend to take very alarmist viewpoints which are then used to justify the draconian measures of the Kyoto Protocol. The IPCC summaries are not science, they are summaries. Furthermore, the predictions made by the IPCC are based on computer models, which have already been shown to be inadequate, and vary widely in their interpretations.

Just as you have noted, Mr. Chairman, as has Senator Craig, the National Research Council recently issued a report called the Science of Research nd Global Change, in that they discussed the abilities of current climate models and here is what they said,

> "The United States today does not have computational and modeling capability needed to serve society's information needs for reliable environmental predictions and projections."

This is what the Clinton administration's Environmental Protection Agency has to say about computer climate models:

> "Virtually all published estimates of how climate change could change in the U.S. are the result of computer models. These complicated models are still not accurate enough to provide a reliable forecast on how climate may change, and several models often yield very contradictory results."

This is from President Clinton's EPA.

We know that the earth's climate has, for thousands of years, gone through cycles of warming and cooling. Ice core samples from Greenland more than 2 miles deep, dating back more than 100,000 years, have shown dramatic fluctuations in the earth's temperature. Since the end of the Ice Age, the last Ice Age 11,000 years ago, when the earth was 12.6 degrees Fahrenheit colder than today, there have been several warming and cooling periods.

Over the last 100 years, surface temperatures have increased by approximately 1 degree Fahrenheit. However, most of that increase in surface temperature occurred before 1940, yet 80 percent of the manmade carbon dioxide was emitted after 1940. Furthermore, while temperatures on the earth's surface have risen slightly over the last two decades, satellite temperatures, which are far more accurate, have shown no warming over the last 20 years.

In fact, from 1979 to 1997, satellite temperatures showed a slight cooling trend of .04 degrees Fahrenheit. Even the scientists most associated with global warming, who we will hear from this morning, Dr. James Hansen, Director of NASA's Goddard Institute for Space Studies, issued a new analysis last year which said the emphasis on carbon dioxide emissions may be misplaced. He will obviously speak for himself, Mr. Chairman.

In 1988, Dr. Hansen testified before a Senate committee that human activities were causing global warming. In his report las August, he found that mandate emissions of carbon dioxide have already been falling. They shrank in 1998 and 1999.

In his report, he stated that other greenhouse gases such as methane, black soot, CFC's, and the compounds that create smog maybe causing more damage than carbon dioxide, and efforts to affect climate change should focus on these other gases because the technology already exists to capture many of them. The prospects for having a modest climate impact instead of disastrous one are quite good, I think, said Dr. Hansen, who was quoted as saying this in the New York Times on August 19, 2000.

Other preeminent climatologists and meteorologists have conducted studies which have offered credible alternatives for the causes of our warming trend. Dr. Sally Belinius, the director of science programs at Harvard's Center for Astrophysics has been able to closely correlate changes in the Sun's brightness with temperature changes on earth. Unlike climate models, her studies have been able to explain why most of the earth's warming in the last 100 years occurred before the significant growth in manmade greenhouse gas emissions. According to her work, solar activity may be the most direct factor in global warming.

Mr. Chairman, we know that we are far from understanding the dynamics of our climate and what stimulates the changes it undergoes. Increasing research and intensifying our scientific effort will help lead us to clear answers to the questions, what is going on, and what is causing it.

In the last Congress, Senators Murkowski, Craig, and I introduced legislation that would dramatically increase funding for research. I would like to thank you, Mr. Chairman and your fellow Commerce Committee members, Senators Dorgan, Brownback, Burns, Smith, others for cosponsoring that legislation. We will be updating and reintroducing this legislation in the next few weeks.

In conclusion, Mr. Chairman, what do we do about climate change? Nothing? No, I do not believe so. None of us have advocated that. That would be irresponsible. However, it would have been equally irresponsible to submit this nation to a treaty that would have had a disastrous effect on our economy without having any real impact on global emissions of greenhouse gases.

President Bush's Interagency Task Force, reviewing climate change, has been listening to and learning from some of the world's foremost meteorologists, climatologists, and scientists in informal meetings. In fact, I believe some of the scientists we hear from this morning have been in those briefings. He has said that the administration will soon offer a relevant, science-based, realistic alternative to the Kyoto treaty. That is the responsible thing to do.

The United States is still a party to the Framework Convention on Climate Change, the Rio treaty, which was signed by the United States and ratified by the U.S. Senate in 1992. We should go back to the framework of that treaty before the Berlin mandate of 1994 that excluded developing countries from participation and laid the groundwork for future international efforts. If we are creative, and our partners will work with us in good faith, we can negotiate arrangements that are responsible, proactive, and realistic.

The United States will need to demonstrate a commitment to act domestically before it will be able to build international support for action absent the Kyoto Protocol. It is in our best interests to create a domestic agenda that will reduce greenhouse gas emissions without the heavy hand of government mandates. A forward-looking domestic policy will demonstrate our commitment, enhance what we genuinely know about climate change, what we do not know about climate change, create more efficient energy sources, and have the additional effect of reducing pollutants.

Mr. Chairman, climate change is a serous issue that deserves serious consideration and, as I stated earlier, our colleagues, Senators Murkowski, Craig, and I, along with others, will soon introduce legislation to improve the scientific knowledge base and lay out positive steps that we can take now to address that change.

I again add my thanks, congratulations to you, your active participation, this Committee's oversight, to this effort. It will take all of us understanding more and more of not just the sound science dynamic of this, but what do we do about it, and how do we apply the resources that we have in this country and in the world to address this issue.

Mr. Chairman, thank you.

The CHAIRMAN. I thank you both, Senator Craig and Senator HAGEL. We appreciate your input, and we look forward to working with you as we address, as you noted, this issue of deep, growing and serious concern on the part of all Americans. Thank you very much for being here today.

Senator Stevens would like to make a comment or remarks before he has to go to another hearing.

STATEMENT OF HON TED STEVENS, U.S. SENATOR FROM ALASKA

Senator STEVENS. Thank you very much, Mr. Chairman. I, too, congratulate you for these hearings.

I have just returned from the Arctic and our people in Alaska, along the Arctic Coast, are very worried about the change that they are observing now, and I intend to take a group of Senators and staff to Alaska over the Memorial Day recess to have hearings in Fairbanks with the International Arctic Research Commission on the question. I wanted to call that to your attention, and those who are here. I hope many Senators will join us.

We have faced the problem of moving Native villages that have been located along the Arctic and West Coast of Alaska for centuries because they are slowly but surely being inundated by sea water. That is true of Point Barrow. I talked to some of my friends who have been out on the ice this year and they tell me that the ice thickness is probably 8 inches thinner this year than it was last year, and that we probably are going to have to move a substantial portion of Point Barrow.

The difficulty is, is that this is a creeping disaster. It is not a disaster—we are not even sure that it is covered by the existing disaster law, but very clearly what I want the Members of the Senate to see along with me and others, and listen to, some of the international people who have been working with the International Arctic Research Commission to try and define what we can expect with regard to the changes in the Arctic.

As you know, the Northwest Passage will be open for the third year in a row. We have observed open needs at the North Pole itself in the Arctic, and I think it is a very serious thing, particularly for my state and the people who live along the coastline of my state. I would be glad to invite any member of the committee who wants to join us.

We intend to stop two or three places and see, actually see the onslaught of the ocean on these people who live along the shore in our state, and then we will listen to some of the people from throughout the Northern Hemisphere and Japan and Canada and the United States, and try to tell us their predictions of what we can expect.

We hope we will get some idea of the timing of the impact on the Arctic, but I do thank you for the time right now, and I would urge any member of this Committee who wants to join us to let us know, because we will be leaving for that period.

There will be hearings in Fairbanks for 2 days right after Memorial Day and before that we will go up and look at the Arctic in two or three places to see what is happening there. Thank you very much for the time.

The CHAIRMAN. I thank you, Senator Stevens, for what you had to say. It argues for taking more action than increasing our modeling capabilities. I thank you, Senator Stevens. I know you have to go.

Our next panel is—would they please come forward?—Dr. Venkatachala Ramaswamy, senior scientist, Geophysical Fluids Dynamics Laboratory, National Oceanic and Atmospheric Administration, henceforward known as NOAA, Dr. James McCarthy, director of the Museum of Comparative Zoology at Harvard University, Dr. Jayant Sathaye, senior scientist at Lawrence Berkeley National Laboratory, University of California, Dr. James Hansen, chief of the Goddard Institute for Space Studies at NASA, and Dr. Richard Lindzen, who is professor at Massachusetts Institute of Technology in Cambridge.

Dr. Ramaswamy.

STATEMENT OF DR. VENKATACHALA RAMASWAMY, SENIOR SCIENTIST, GEOPHYSICAL FLUIDS DYNAMICS LABORATORY, NATIONAL OCEANIC AND ATMOSPHERIC ADMINISTRATION

Dr. RAMASWAMY. Mr. Chairman and members of the committee, good morning. My name is Venkatachala Ramaswamy. I appreciate the invitation to appear before your Committee and give a report on the state of the scientific understanding of global climate change, as documented in the recently concluded IPCC report. Copies of the summary for policymakers and technical summary have been distributed, as has been the verbal testimony with its appendix.

Just a brief word about the assessment. The assessment took almost 3 years in preparation, between 1998 and 2001, and represents the work of over 100 scientific authors as well as several hundred contributing authors worldwide. It is based on peer-reviewed scientific literature and was carefully scrutinized by hundreds of scientific peers through an extensive review process.

I was a coordinating lead author for one of the chapters. There were 14 chapters in all. I was coordinating lead author of one of the chapters, and also a member of the drafting team of the summary for policymakers, which carefully went through the science contained in the summary. My testimony today summarizes the understanding as it is manifested in the various chapters of the report, and as summarized in the summary for policymakers.

Before starting on the scientific findings of the new report, I would like to begin with the reiteration of a fundamental long-standing knowledge, namely, that (1) there is a natural greenhouse effect which keeps the earth warmer than it would be otherwise, and (2) greenhouse gases are increasing in the atmosphere because of human activities, and they are increasingly trapping more heat in the climate system.

There are many agents which force climate change, and these factors are greenhouse gas concentrations, tropospheric aerosols, the sun's energy output, land use change, and the explosive episodic volcanic eruptions which lead to transitory increases in stratospheric aerosols.

The characteristics of these forcings can be summarized as: the long-lived gases have a forcing which is global in extent, that is, they exert a forcing all over the globe; this is in contrast to short-lived species, for example, ozone and aerosols, which vary considerably with region and season. Sun and volcanoes are natural forcing factors.

One characteristic stands out from the assessment of the forcings, which is that the estimate and the level of scientific understanding of greenhouse gases forcing is greater than for other forcings.

Before discussing the effects of these agents on climate change, let us state what has the actual climate undergone and what are our observations of the climate system? Well, the measurements suggest that there is a growing collective picture of a warming world over the past century. The global-mean surface temperatures are up .4 to .8 degrees Celsius over the past 100 years. In the hand-out, there is a diagram showing the Northern Hemisphere surface temperatures, culled from the last 140 years, using instrumental record and, then, prior to that, using proxy records. It shows the degree of rapid increase of temperatures over the last century compared to both the mean and the variability expressed on the curve.

Along with the global warming, there have been other changes which are consistent with this picture, namely the retreat of mountain glaciers in nonpolar regions, decrease in the amount of snow cover, the rise in the global average sea level by 4 to 8 inches.

What are the causes of the observed warming? To analyze this issue, IPCC resorts to model simulations. Based on analysis of both the observed record and climate model simulations using the various forcing agents, it is seen that there is now new and stronger evidence that most of the observed warming over the past 50 years is attributable to human activities.

This is based on the fact there is a better simulation of the instrumental temperature record when all the forcings, natural and human-related, are taken into consideration. Only natural forcings do not lead to a good agreement with the observations. Neither does the internal variability of the climate system, as estimated by models, explain the rise in temperature.

The key factors since the 1995 IPCC report are that there is now 5 years of additional data which shows a rapid increase of warming; and the new 1,000-year record, which is based on proxy data now extending prior to 140 years ago, and that sets up a context for the changes over the past century. Also, climate models have evolved and improved since the last IPCC report.

So now the question is, what could all of this mean for the future? IPCC considered a range of mission scenarios, and although the abundances of various greenhouse gases and aerosols in the future cannot be predicted with a high degree of confidence, IPCC considered a suite of possible futures based on considerations of economies, populations, et cetera.

The conclusion from model calculations of the responses to these various scenarios is that a continued growth in greenhouse gases is projected to lead to very significant increases in global mean temperatures and sea level. As far as numbers are concerned, by 2100 the global mean surface temperature is projected to increase by 2½ to 10 degrees Fahrenheit, considering the range of scenarios, and considering the modeling uncertainties.

The projected rate of warming from these model simulations is very likely to be larger than changes that have been observed over the past 10,000 years. Along with the global-mean surface temperature change, there is a corresponding projected sea level rise due to thermal expansion of sea water, on the order of 4 to 35 inches.

Climate changes in specific regions and years cannot be predicted with a high degree of confidence but it is likely that there would be a shift of the climate to a new regime, and it is likely that the weather could be more variable.

Amidst these projections, a key feature to be borne in mind, one which has been stated in the earlier IPCC reports and which is worth reiterating here today, is that the greenhouse warming can be reversed only very slowly. This is because of one, the slow rate of removal of many of the gases from the atmosphere—for example,

CO_2—because they have long lifetimes, and second, the slow response of oceans to thermal perturbations.

Finally, Mr. Chairman, I would like to conclude with an important remark concerning the IPCC report. This climate science assessment is the considered viewpoint of hundreds of scientists worldwide, and is based upon the research results of the worldwide community that are published in numerous peer-reviewed scientific journals; there are some 4,000 references that are referred to in the Working Group 1 report on the science.

The resulting report contains policy-relevant scientific information but, of course, makes no policy statements or recommendations. I will conclude by thanking you for the invitation to appear today, and to report the findings of the Working Group 1 on the scientific understanding of global climate change.

I hope this summary has been helpful to you, Mr. Chairman, and to the committee. I would be happy to address any questions. Thank you very much.

[The prepared statement of Dr. Ramaswamy follows:]

PREPARED STATEMENT OF DR. VENKATACHALA RAMASWAMY, SENIOR SCIENTIST, GEOPHYSICAL FLUID DYNAMICS LABORATORY, NATIONAL OCEANIC AND ATMOSPHERIC ADMINISTRATION

Mr. Chairman: I am a Senior Scientist at NOAA's Geophysical Fluid Dynamics Laboratory located in Princeton University, Princeton, New Jersey. I appreciate the invitation to appear before your Committee and report on the state of the scientific understanding of global climate change as documented in the recently concluded Intergovernmental Panel on Climate Change (IPCC) assessment ["Climate Change 2001: The Scientific Basis"]. The IPCC was set up by the World Meteorological Organization (WMO) and the United Nations Environment Program (UNEP) to provide expert assessment of the knowledge and an authoritative international statement of the scientific understanding on climate change.

For over 30 years, the Geophysical Fluid Dynamics Laboratory has been a world leader in the development of numerical models for studying climate variations and climate change, and has made major contributions to the understanding of the Earth's climate system. My own research has involved estimating the natural and human-induced factors that force climate change, as well as investigating the manner in which the climate system responds to these factors. For over a decade, I have been involved in various national and international scientific assessments. These include National Academy of Science studies, WMO/UNEP reports on the scientific understanding of the ozone layer and IPCC climate change science assessments. In the recently concluded IPCC scientific assignment, I served as the Coordinating Lead Author for the Chapter on "Radiative Forcing of Climate Change." I was also a member of the panel which drafted the Summary for Policymakers that was formally approved in detail and accepted along with the underlying assessment report at the IPCC Working Group I Plenary session in January 2001.

I appreciate the invitation to summarize the findings from the IPCC (2001) report. My information is based on the set of findings in this report. The assessment took almost three years in preparation and represents the work of over a hundred scientific authors worldwide. It is based on scientific literature, and was carefully scrutinized by hundreds of scientific peers through an extensive peer review process. My testimony today summarizes the understanding of these authors as manifested in the report.

Before addressing the new findings of the recent report, two fundamental points are worthy of note. These have been long-known, are very well understood, and have been deeply underscored in all previous IPCC reports and other such scientific summaries.

• *The "greenhouse" effect is real, and is an essential component of the planet's climate process.* A small percentage (roughly 2%) of the atmosphere is, and long has been, composed of greenhouse gases (water vapor, carbon dioxide, ozone and methane). These effectively prevent part of the heat radiated by the Earth's surface from otherwise escaping to space. The global system responds to this trapped heat with a climate that is warmer, on the average, than it would be otherwise without the presence of these gases.

In addition to the natural greenhouse effect above, there is a change underway in the greenhouse radiation balance, namely:

• *Some greenhouse gases are increasing in the atmosphere because of human activities and increasingly trapping more heat.* Direct atmospheric measurements made over the past 40-plus years have documented the steady growth in the atmospheric abundance of carbon dioxide. In addition to these direct real-time measurements, ice cores have revealed the atmospheric carbon dioxide concentrations of the distant past. Measurements using the air bubbles that were trapped within the layers of accumulating snow show that atmospheric carbon dioxide has increased by more than 30% over the Industrial Era (since 1750), compared to the relatively constant abundance that it had over the preceding 750 years of the past millennium [see Figure 2, IPCC Working Group I Summary for Policymakers, page 6]. The predominant cause of this increase in carbon dioxide is the combustion of fossil fuels and the burning of forests. Further, methane abundance has doubled over the Industrial Era. Other heat-trapping gases are also increasing as a result of human activities.

The increase in greenhouse gas concentrations in the atmosphere implies a positive radiative forcing, i.e., a tendency to warm the climate system [see Figure 3, IPCC Working Group I Summary for Policymakers, 2001; page 8]. Particles (or aerosols) in the atmosphere resulting from human activities can also affect climate. Aerosols vary considerably by region. Some aerosol types act in a sense opposite to the greenhouse gases and cause a negative forcing or cooling of the climate system (e.g., sulfate aerosol), while others act in the same sense and warm the climate (e.g., soot). In contrast to the long-lived nature of carbon dioxide (centuries), aerosols are short-lived and removed from the lower atmosphere relatively quickly (within a few days). Therefore, aerosols exert a long-term forcing on climate only because their emissions continue each year. In summary, emissions of greenhouse gases and aerosols due to human activities continue to alter the atmosphere in ways that are expected to affect the climate. There are also natural factors which exert a forcing of climate, e.g., changes in the Sun's energy output and short-lived (about 1 to 2 years) aerosols in the stratosphere following episodic and explosive volcanic eruptions. IPCC evaluated the state of the knowledge and assessed the level of scientific understanding of each forcing. The level of understanding and the forcing estimate in the case of the greenhouse gases are greater than for other forcing agents.

What do these changes in the forcing agents mean for changes in the climate system? What climate changes have been observed? How well are the causes of those changes understood? Namely, what are changes due to natural factors, and what are changes due to the greenhouse-gas increases? And, what does this understanding potentially imply about the climate of the future?

These questions bear directly on the scientific points that you have asked me to address today. In doing so, findings emerging from the recent IPCC climate science report with respect to measurements, analyses of climate change to date, and projections of climate change will be summarized.

• *There is a growing set of observations that yields a collective picture of a warming world over the past century.* The global-average surface temperature has increased over the 20th century by 0.7 to 1.4 degrees Fahrenheit [See Figure 1, IPCC Working Group I Summary for Policymakers, 2001, page 3]. The average temperature increase in the Northern Hemisphere over the 20th century is likely to have been the largest of any century during the past 1,000 years, based on "proxy" data (and their uncertainties) from tree rings, corals, ice cores, and historical records. Other observed changes are consistent with this warming. There has been a widespread retreat of mountain glaciers in non-polar regions. Snow cover and ice extent have decreased. The global-average sea level has risen between 4 and 8 inches, which is consistent with a warmer ocean occupying more space because of the thermal expansion of sea water and loss of land ice.

• *There is new and stronger evidence that most of the warming observed over the last 50 years is attributable to human activities.* The 1995 IPCC climate-science assessment report concluded: "The balance of evidence suggests a discernible human influence on global climate." There is now a longer and more closely scrutinized observed temperature record. Climate models have evolved and improved significantly since the last assessment. Although many of the sources of uncertainty identified in 1995 still remain to some degree, new evidence and improved understanding support the updated conclusion. Namely, recent analyses have compared the surface temperatures measured over the last 140 years to those simulated by mathematical models of the climate system, thereby evaluating the degree to which human influences can be detected. Both natural climate-change agents (solar variation and episodic, explosive volcanic eruptions) and human-related agents (greenhouse gases and fine particles) were included. The natural climate-change agents alone do not explain the warming in the second half of the 20th century. The best agreement between observations and model simulations over the last 140 years is found when both human-related and natural climate-change agents are included in the simulations [see Figure 4, IPCC Working Group I Summary for Policymakers, 2001; page 11]. Further, model simulations indicate that the warming over the past century is very unlikely to be due to internal variability alone, i.e., variations within the climate system that would be expected even in the absence of any forcing. In light of such new evidence and taking into account the remaining uncertainties, the IPCC scientists concluded that most of the observed warming over the last 50 years is likely to have been due to the increase in greenhouse gas concentrations.

• *Scenarios of future human activities indicate continued changes in atmospheric composition throughout the 21st century.* The atmospheric abundances of greenhouse gases and aerosols over the next 100 years cannot be predicted with high confidence, since the future emissions of these species will depend on many diverse factors, e.g., world population, economies, technologies, and human choices, which are not uniquely specifiable. Rather, the IPCC assessment endeavor aimed at establishing a set of scenarios of greenhouse gas and aerosol abundances, with each based on a picture of what the world plausibly could be over the 21st century. [The emission scenarios were based on the IPCC Special Report on Emissions Scenarios, 2000; a brief description of the scenarios appears in the box on page 18 of the Summary for Policymakers report.] Based on these scenarios and the estimated uncertainties in climate models, the resulting projection for the global average temperature increase by the year 2100 ranges from 2.5 to 10 degrees Fahrenheit [see Figure 5, IPCC Working Group I Summary for Policymakers, 2001; page 14]. Such a projected rate of warming would be much larger than the observed 20th-century changes and would very likely be without precedent during at least the last 10,000 years. The corresponding projected increase in global sea level by the end of this century ranges from 3.5 to 35 inches. Uncertainties in the understanding of some climate processes make it more difficult to project meaningfully the corresponding changes in regional climate.

Finally, I would like to relate a basic scientific aspect, one that has been underscored with very high confidence in all of the IPCC climate-science assessment reports (1990, 1995, and 2001). It is repeated here because it is a key (perhaps "the" key) aspect of a greenhouse-gas-induced climate change:

• *A greenhouse-gas warming could be reversed only very slowly.* This quasi-irreversibility arises because of the slow rate of removal (centuries) from the atmosphere of many of the greenhouse gases and because of the slow response of the oceans to thermal changes. For example, several centuries after carbon dioxide emissions occur, about a quarter of the increase in the atmospheric concentrations caused by these emissions is projected to still be in the atmosphere. Additionally, global average temperature increases and rising sea level are projected to continue for hundreds of years after a stabilization of greenhouse gas concentrations (including a stabilization at today's abundances), owing to the long timescales (centuries) on which the deep ocean adjusts to climate change.

Let me conclude, Mr. Chairman, with an important remark concerning the IPCC report. As noted, the IPCC climate-science assessment is the considered viewpoint of hundreds of scientists worldwide. This assessment is based upon the research results of the worldwide community that are published in numerous peer-reviewed scientific journals. The resulting report contains policy-relevant scientific information, but makes no policy statements or recommendations. As such, the three components of the 2001 IPCC Third Assessment Report—climate science, impacts, and mitigation—are recommended as a key information source that is available to the Committee as it continues this important dialogue about climate change and its relation to humankind.

Thank you for the invitation to appear today. I hope that this summary has been useful. I would be happy to address any questions.

Variations of the Earth's surface temperature for:

(a) the past 140 years

GLOBAL

Data from thermometers.

(b) the past 1,000 years

NORTHERN HEMISPHERE

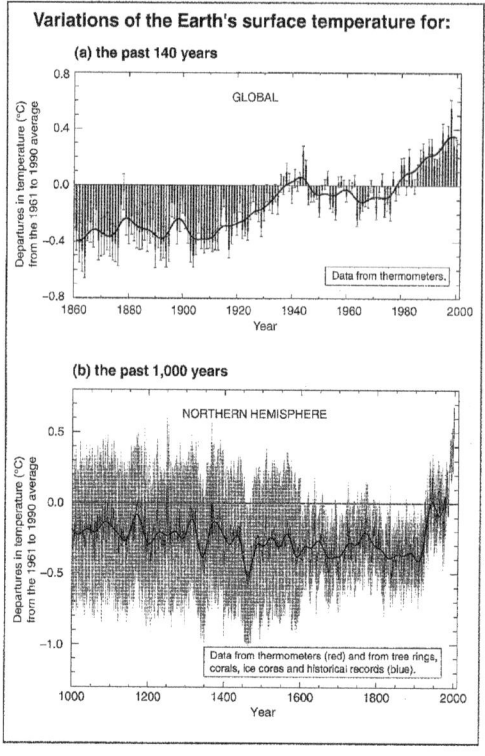

Data from thermometers (red) and from tree rings, corals, ice cores and historical records (blue).

Figure 1: Variations of the Earth's surface temperature over the last 140 years and the last millennium.

(a) The Earth's surface temperature is shown year by year (red bars) and approximately decade by decade (black line, a filtered annual curve suppressing fluctuations below near decadal time-scales). There are uncertainties in the annual data (thin black whisker bars represent the 95% confidence range) due to data gaps, random instrumental errors and uncertainties, uncertainties in bias corrections in the ocean surface temperature data and also in adjustments for urbanisation over the land. Over both the last 140 years and 100 years, the best estimate is that the global average surface temperature has increased by 0.6 ± 0.2°C.

(b) Additionally, the year by year (blue curve) and 50 year average (black curve) variations of the average surface temperature of the Northern Hemisphere for the past 1000 years have been reconstructed from "proxy" data calibrated against thermometer data (see list of the main proxy data in the diagram). The 95% confidence range in the annual data is represented by the grey region. These uncertainties increase in more distant times and are always much larger than in the instrumental record due to the use of relatively sparse proxy data. Nevertheless the rate and duration of warming of the 20th century has been much greater than in any of the previous nine centuries. Similarly, it is likely[7] that the 1990s have been the warmest decade and 1998 the warmest year of the millennium.

[Based upon (a) Chapter 2, Figure 2.7c and (b) Chapter 2, Figure 2.20]

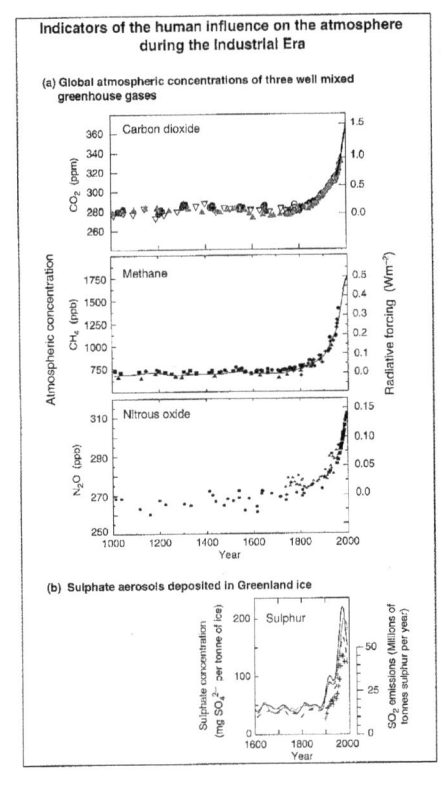

Figure 2: Long records of past changes in atmospheric composition provide the context for the influence of anthropogenic emissions.

(a) shows changes in the atmospheric concentrations of carbon dioxide (CO_2), methane (CH_4), and nitrous oxide (N_2O) over the past 1000 years. The ice core and firn data for several sites in Antarctica and Greenland (shown by different symbols) are supplemented with the data from direct atmospheric samples over the past few decades (shown by the line for CO_2 and incorporated in the curve representing the global average of CH_4). The estimated positive radiative forcing of the climate system from these gases is indicated on the right-hand scale. Since these gases have atmospheric lifetimes of a decade or more, they are well mixed, and their concentrations reflect emissions from sources throughout the globe. All three records show effects of the large and increasing growth in anthropogenic emissions during the Industrial Era.

(b) illustrates the influence of industrial emissions on atmospheric sulphate concentrations, which produce negative radiative forcing. Shown is the time history of the concentrations of sulphate, not in the atmosphere but in ice cores in Greenland (shown by lines; from which the episodic effects of volcanic eruptions have been removed). Such data indicate the local deposition of sulphate aerosols at the site, reflecting sulphur dioxide (SO_2) emissions at mid-latitudes in the Northern Hemisphere. This record, albeit more regional than that of the globally-mixed greenhouse gases, demonstrates the large growth in anthropogenic SO_2 emissions during the Industrial Era. The pluses denote the relevant regional estimated SO_2 emissions (right-hand scale).

[Based upon (a) Chapter 3, Figure 3.2b (CO_2); Chapter 4, Figure 4.1a and b (CH_4) and Chapter 4, Figure 4.2 (N_2O) and (b) Chapter 5, Figure 5.4a]

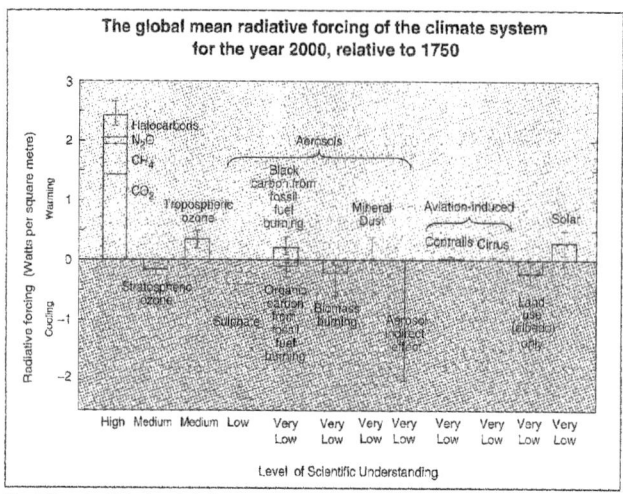

Figure 3: Many external factors force climate change.

These radiative forcings arise from changes in the atmospheric composition, alteration of surface reflectance by land use, and variation in the output of the sun. Except for solar variation, some form of human activity is linked to each. The rectangular bars represent estimates of the contributions of these forcings – some of which yield warming, and some cooling. Forcing due to episodic volcanic events, which lead to a negative forcing lasting only for a few years, is not shown. The indirect effect of aerosols shown is their effect on the size and number of cloud droplets. A second indirect effect of aerosols on clouds, namely their effect on cloud lifetime, which would also lead to a negative forcing, is not shown. Effects of aviation on greenhouse gases are included in the individual bars. The vertical line about the rectangular bars indicates a range of estimates, guided by the spread in the published values of the forcings and physical understanding. Some of the forcings possess a much greater degree of certainty than others. A vertical line without a rectangular bar denotes a forcing for which no best estimate can be given owing to large uncertainties. The overall level of scientific understanding for each forcing varies considerably, as noted. Some of the radiative forcing agents are well mixed over the globe, such as CO_2, thereby perturbing the global heat balance. Others represent perturbations with stronger regional signatures because of their spatial distribution, such as aerosols. For this and other reasons, a simple sum of the positive and negative bars cannot be expected to yield the net effect on the climate system. The simulations of this assessment report (for example, Figure 5) indicate that the estimated net effect of these perturbations is to have warmed the global climate since 1750. [Based upon Chapter 6, Figure 6.6]

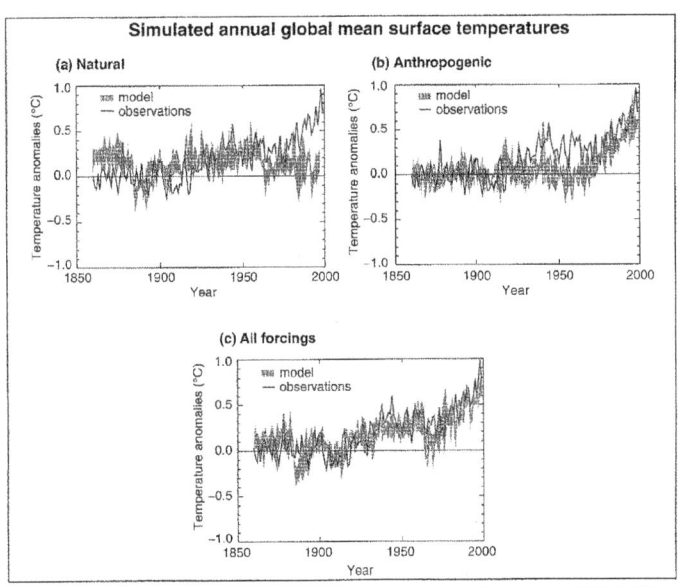

Figure 4: Simulating the Earth's temperature variations, and comparing the results to measured changes, can provide insight into the underlying causes of the major changes.

A climate model can be used to simulate the temperature changes that occur both from natural and anthropogenic causes. The simulations represented by the band in (a) were done with only natural forcings: solar variation and volcanic activity. Those encompassed by the band in (b) were done with anthropogenic forcings: greenhouse gases and an estimate of sulphate aerosols, and those encompassed by the band in (c) were done with both natural and anthropogenic forcings included. From (b), it can be seen that inclusion of anthropogenic forcings provides a plausible explanation for a substantial part of the observed temperature changes over the past century, but the best match with observations is obtained in (c) when both natural and anthropogenic factors are included. These results show that the forcings included are sufficient to explain the observed changes, but do not exclude the possibility that other forcings may also have contributed. The bands of model results presented here are for four runs from the same model. Similar results to those in (b) are obtained with other models with anthropogenic forcing. [Based upon Chapter 12, Figure 12.7]

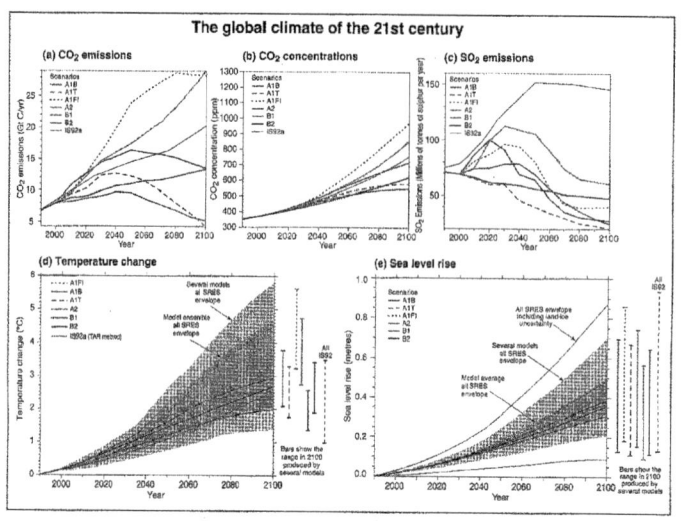

Figure 5: The global climate of the 21st century will depend on natural changes and the response of the climate system to human activities.

Climate models project the response of many climate variables – such as increases in global surface temperature and sea level – to various scenarios of greenhouse gas and other human-related emissions. (a) shows the CO_2 emissions of the six illustrative SRES scenarios, which are summarised in the box on page 18, along with IS92a for comparison purposes with the SAR. (b) shows projected CO_2 concentrations. (c) shows anthropogenic SO_2 emissions. Emissions of other gases and other aerosols were included in the model but are not shown in the figure. (d) and (e) show the projected temperature and sea level responses, respectively. The "several models all SRES envelope" in (d) and (e) shows the temperature and sea level rise, respectively, for the simple model when tuned to a number of complex models with a range of climate sensitivities. All SRES envelopes refer to the full range of 35 SRES scenarios. The "model average all SRES envelope" shows the average from these models for the range of scenarios. Note that the warming and sea level rise from these emissions would continue well beyond 2100. Also note that this range does not allow for uncertainty relating to ice dynamical changes in the West Antarctic ice sheet, nor does it account for uncertainties in projecting non-sulphate aerosols and greenhouse gas concentrations. [Based upon (a) Chapter 3, Figure 3.12, (b) Chapter 3, Figure 3.12, (c) Chapter 5, Figure 5.13, (d) Chapter 9, Figure 9.14, (e) Chapter 11, Figure 11.12, Appendix II]

The CHAIRMAN. Thank you very much.
Dr. McCarthy, welcome.

STATEMENT OF JAMES J. McCARTHY, DIRECTOR, MUSEUM OF COMPARATIVE ZOOLOGY, HARVARD UNIVERSITY

Dr. MCCARTHY. Thank you. Good morning, Mr. Chairman, and members. I am James McCarthy, professor of biological oceanography at Harvard University, where I am also the director of the Museum of Comparative Zoology, and I also head our undergraduate program on environmental science and public policy, but the reason I am here today, of course, is in my capacity as the co-chair of the Intergovernmental Panel on Climate Change Working Group 2. I and a colleague, Osvaldo Canziani, a meteorologist from Argentina, have co-chaired this Working Group.

The charge of this Working Group was to assess evidence for impacts, adaptations and vulnerabilities associated with climate change. We began this assessment in the autumn of 1997, and concluded it earlier this spring.

Mr. Chairman, I read the testimony related to climate change submitted to your Committee last year on three occasions, May, July, and September. In each case for which evidence of climate change impacts were cited, we now have greater confidence that these effects are widespread and more conclusively linked to climate change.

Some witnesses presented evidence of no change in climate, or absence of climate change impacts. In my judgment it was the selection of data for a particular region or particular time period that led them to these conclusions. This, Mr. Chairman, is why the work of the IPCC is so important. Some nations have sponsored and will continue to sponsor studies that may show, quite correctly, that recent data for their localities do not show evidence of change. The IPCC focus is on broad patterns and generalizations that arise from these patterns.

Dr. Neil Lane reported to you that 89 of 99 plants examined in the District of Columbia are blooming a full week earlier now than they did a mere 30 years ago, but is this true everywhere in the globe? Probably not. Were a survey in some other city to reveal no such change, would this cause one to doubt that there had been change in Washington, DC.? Certainly, it would not.

From the IPCC assessment, what is now clear is that this type of effect in plants and animals over the last few decades is evident on all continents, and in 80 percent of the published cases, the change in the distribution of animals or their biology is consistent with local changes in temperature. This is strong evidence of biological response to climate change.

So, we have already seen effects of recent climate change in ecosystems. While none of these might be classified as dangerous per se, it is unlikely that they will be reversed within our lifetime by any action that we might take today to reduce the rate of climate change. And the rate of climate change projected for the 21st Century, as we have just heard from my colleague, is, on average, 2 to 10 times the rate observed in the 20th Century.

In all likelihood, this projected change will lead to displacements of species, and perhaps extinctions, especially in tropical ocean and arctic ecosystems such as we were just hearing from Senator Stevens. But for the lives and livelihood of humankind, the largest associated effects of these shifts in organisms will be in regional agricultural productivity, and in distribution of disease organisms and their vectors. North American and Northern Eurasian agriculture may, in fact, be enhanced, albeit with a northward shift. However, the tropical and subtropical regions will be hardest hit, with potentially serious losses of agricultural capacity.

Human systems other than agriculture are also being affected by climate change, some from general warming, such as with human health, but others from an increasing frequency, intensity, and persistence of extreme events.

If climate change is steady and smooth, most of it may be accommodated or adapted to without great cost, but if the path is bumpy the story becomes very different. There is no good news in extreme events. These are inherently disruptive, and one need only look at the last 5 years to see the global evidence of this, with floods and mudslides of unprecedented proportion in Honduras in 1998, where more than 10,000 lives were lost, and Venezuela in 1999, where more than 25,0000 lives were lost, and on other continents as well, in Africa, with Mozambique and Kenya, in Asia with China and North Korea.

Our report, Mr. Chairman, summarizes our assessment of the published literature on the likely effects of projected changes in climate on a suite of systems and economic sectors, and for eight broad regions of the globe we identify the most serious vulnerabilities. The tropical and subtropical regions, many of them already water-stressed and facing serious questions of food security, will be hardest hit. This disproportionate impact is in no small part because these regions, many with developing countries, are poorly equipped to adapt. In many cases they lack the infrastructure and simple resources such as in the case of public health measures. But it is also incorrect to assume that northern industrialized nations will be spared serious effects of climate change within their own sovereign territories. The fraction of their citizens who are most vulnerable to heat waves, floods, and droughts, will increase.

In summary, Mr. Chairman, some of the climate changes projected for the future have positive effects: less human winter mortality in some regions, enhanced crop growth in others, for example, but most systems and most sectors and most people will be adversely affected by this climate change. For most people, the projected rate of change will simply exceed capacities to adapt to even gradual change, let alone a future with more frequent, intense, and persistent extreme events.

Our report calls attention to the need to explore all opportunities to reduce potential adverse effects of climate change by enhancing adaptive capacity, as with some of the issues that were being addressed by Senator Stevens.

Thank you again, Mr. Chairman, for this opportunity to present some of our results to your Committee. I realize that in addition to the results of the assessment themselves, you and members of your Committee may have some questions about the methods and procedures of the IPCC. I refer here specifically to the last portion of my submitted testimony, in which I discussed the actual preparation of the Summary for Policymakers and, with all due respect, I think Senator Hagel has been misinformed as to how this actually occurs.

In my written testimony, I have remarked on this process, and I will be happy to discuss further any aspect of the findings of either the procedures of the IPCC Working Group 2, or its results, as you wish.

Thank you.

[The prepared statement of Dr. McCarthy follows:]

PREPARED STATEMENT OF JAMES J. MCCARTHY, DIRECTOR,
MUSEUM OF COMPARATIVE ZOOLOGY, HARVARD UNIVERSITY

Thank you, Senator McCain, for this opportunity to address the Committee on Commerce, Science, and Transportation. My name is James J. McCarthy, and I am a Professor of Oceanography, the Director of the Museum of Comparative Zoology, and the Head Tutor for undergraduate students studying Environmental Science and Public Policy at Harvard University.

For nearly four years I have co-chaired Working Group II (WG II) of the Intergovernmental Panel on Climate Change (IPCC). The focus of this working group has been to assess potential impacts, adaptations, and vulnerabilities to climate change. In my letter of invitation to this hearing you have asked that I comment on the results and conclusions of the IPCC WG II and other related issues that I wish to bring to the attention of the Committee.

The new WG II report, *Climate Change 2001: Impacts, Adaptation, and Vulnerability*, is the most comprehensive and up-to-date scientific assessment of the consequences of, and adaptation responses to, climate change. The report:

• evaluates evidence that recent observed changes in climate have already affected a variety of physical and biological systems.

• makes a detailed study of the vulnerabilities of human populations to future climate change, including associated sea-level rise and changes in the frequency and intensity of climate extremes such as floods, droughts, heat waves and windstorms, and taking into account potential impacts on water resources, agriculture and food security, human health, coastal and other types of settlements, and economic activities.

• assesses the potential responses of natural environments and the wildlife that inhabit them to future climate change and identifies environments at particular risk.

• considers how adaptation to climate change might lessen adverse impacts or enhance beneficial impacts.

• provides an overview of the vulnerabilities and adaptation possibilities by major region of the world (Africa, Asia, Australia/New Zealand, Europe, Latin America, Polar Regions, and Small Island States).

• contrasts the different vulnerabilities of the developed and developing parts of the world and explores the implications for sustainable development and equity concerns.

Research on climate impacts has grown considerably during the five years since the last IPCC assessment, and much has been learned regarding the potential risk of damage associated with projected climate change. In particular, this research has added new understanding of vulnerabilities to climate change across a spectrum of ecological systems (forests, grasslands, wetlands, rivers, lakes and marine environments) and human systems (agriculture, water resources, coastal resources, human health, financial institutions, and human settlements).

Observational evidence of changes has accumulated in many physical and biological systems (*e.g.* glacial melting, shifts in geographic ranges of plant and animal species, and changes in plant and animal biology) that are highly consistent with warming observed in recent decades. These observations are adding to our knowledge of the sensitivity of affected systems to changes in climate and can help us to understand the vulnerability of systems to the greater and more rapid climate changes projected for the 21st century. A number of unique systems are increasingly recognized as especially vulnerable to climate change (*e.g.* glaciers, coral reefs and atolls, mangroves, boreal and tropical forests, polar and alpine ecosystems, prairie wetlands, and remnant native grasslands). In addition, climate change is expected to threaten some species with greater probability of extinction. Potential changes in the frequency, intensity, and persistence of climate extremes (e.g. heat waves, heavy precipitation, and drought) and in climate variability (e.g. El Niño—Southern Oscillation) are emerging as key determinants of future impacts and vulnerability. The many interactions of climate change with other stresses on the environment and human populations, as well as linkages between climate change and sustainable development, are increasingly emphasized in recent research and preliminary insights from these important efforts are reflected in the report.

The value of adaptation measures to diminish the risk of damage from future climate change, and from present climate variability, was recognized in previous assessments and is confirmed and expanded upon in the new assessment. Understanding of the determinants of adaptive capacity has advanced and confirms the conclusion that developing countries, particularly the least developed countries, have lesser capacity to adapt than do developed countries. This condition results in relatively high vulnerability to damaging effects of climate change in these countries.

MORE SPECIFIC NEW FINDINGS

The effects of recent climate change are now clearly evident in many natural systems. Changes in the distribution of species as documented in the fossil record have long been used as an important diagnostic of past climate. In addition, it is well known that the seasonal behavior of many species, such as migrations and reproductive behavior (e.g. flowering time and egg laying) are sensitive to temperature. In the past few decades substantial changes in these characteristics have been noted for many species, and for 80% of the cases for which such changes could plausibly be linked to temperature, the biotic changes were consistent with changes in regional temperature.

The documented changes in Arctic sea ice cover, both its thinning and its shrinkage during summer, affect polar ecosystems. The shrinkage that is occurring has averaged 3% per decade for the entire Arctic over the last three decades. Throughout Northern Hemisphere freshwater ecosystems the ice-free season is now nearly 2 weeks longer than it was a century ago, which is consistent with an average annual temperature increase of about $1°C$. Increased access for ships is a positive aspect of this trend. During the summer of 2000, for the first time in recorded history, a RCMP ship transited the Northwest Passage without touching ice. With summer ice-free conditions in the Arctic expanding poleward, ecosystems will shift accordingly. Marine mammals, such as walrus, certain seals, and the polar bear have evolved with a dependence on ice for successful feeding and rearing of their young. As summer ice retreats from land earlier in the season and reaches greater maximum distances, the success of these species will be challenged. Now, in the span of a single human generation, observations point to a coherent shift in the pattern of temperature sensitive systems on all continents.

Many human systems are also inherently sensitive to climate change. Examples in the IPCC report include:
• changes in potential crop yields, especially reductions in most tropical and subtropical regions.
• changes in water availability, especially losses in the sub-tropics.
• an increase in the number of people exposed to vector born diseases like malaria and water borne diseases like cholera.
• increased losses of lives, livelihood, and property from heavy rains and sea level rise.

Already the increased frequency and intensity of extreme precipitation events has taken a heavy toll. Devastation caused by floods and mudslides in tropical to temperate regions on all continents in the last decade has been without precedent. While a gradual increase in temperature might be accommodated by many natural and human systems, the projected increases in frequency, intensity, and persistence of extreme events has the potential to be enormously disruptive. Moreover the impacts of these changes will fall disproportionately on the poorest peoples. While this may be an obvious conclusion when comparing certain developed and developing countries, it will also be true within a developed country. The fraction of the population that is vulnerable to an extreme heat wave or flood will increase with the severity of the extreme event.

Many of the most devastating aspects of climate change will occur in tropical and subtropical regions, where 70% of the world's population live, many in developing countries. These are the regions that will be the most water stressed, suffer the greatest potential losses of agricultural capacity, and be most vulnerable to the expanded ranges of certain infectious diseases. Even allowing for possible benefits from climate change in some temperate regions, such as net gains in potential crop yields, the negative aspects of climate change in subtropical and tropical regions are likely to offset these positive aspects even assuming there would be no infrastructure or financial obstacle to the distribution of resources, i.e. food, moved from one region to another.

Thus the following are evident in the recent IPCC assessment:
- responses to climate change are already occurring in natural and human systems.
- it is highly likely that climate changes in the 21st century will be 2—10 faster than those of the 19th century.
- increased frequency and severity of extreme events will be costly to natural and human systems.

Given the inertia in human system-climate system linkages, these findings lead inevitably to the conclusion that even the most optimistic scenarios for mitigating future climate change are unlikely to prevent significant damage from occurring. This is not to say that mitigation efforts such as a fully implemented Kyoto Protocol won't be effective; rather that their effect won't be evident for decades. Thus, an important finding of the IPCC is that adaptation will be absolutely necessary to minimize damage that is projected from future climate change. Limitations in adaptive capacity will make some regions and some peoples of lesser means more vulnerable to the impacts of climate change. Natural systems will be affected in all regions from polar to tropical on all continents. Human systems will, however, be most vulnerable to climate change in Africa, Latin America, and Asia where current adaptive capacity is low.

If we wish to minimize the loss of lives, livelihoods and property that will occur during our inevitable transition to a warmer world, it is imperative that we redouble efforts to both minimize the emissions of fossil fuel combustion products and prepare peoples and systems as best we can for the disruption that will ensue with the climate change that is now projected for the 21st century.

COMMENTS ON THE IPCC PROCESS

Nowhere can one find a process that produces a report on the understanding of a broad area of science that is more inclusive in its coverage of contemporary scientific views, or more broadly vetted by the scholarly community than with the IPCC. The basis of the assessment is the peer-reviewed published scientific literature. Every effort is made to be thorough, and serious attention is given to disparate results and conclusions in this literature. To the extent possible, degrees of likelihood are assigned to summary statements, especially those on projected climate conditions and climate impacts.

Currently about 100 governments participate in the IPCC, and all were invited to propose the names of experts who could serve as authors of this report. More than one thousand nominations were received for WG II authors, with supporting documentation listing the nominees' publications in scientific journals. It should be noted that the authors of IPCC reports work without financial compensation for their efforts on behalf of the IPCC.

The report of WG II was drafted between July 1998 and February 2001 by 183 Lead Authors. In addition, 243 Contributing Authors, from nearly 70 countries, submitted draft text and information to the Lead Authors. Drafts of the report were circulated twice for review, first to experts and a second time to both experts and governments. Comments received from 440 reviewers were carefully analyzed and assimilated in a revised the document, with guidance provided by 33 Review Editors. The full report was then condensed into a 70-page manuscript, known as a Technical Summary (TS), and it was then further condensed into a 20-page manuscript known as a Summary for Policy Makers (SPM). The TS and SPM (along with a revision of the full report that reflected the earlier government and expert review) were then sent out for a final review coordinated by governments.

Comments from this final review were then used to prepare a revision of the SPM and TS, and a plenary of the Working Group was convened to consider final approval of the SPM. This involved about 150 delegates from 100 nations, drawn from each nation's departments and ministries of state and science. The plenary met for four days in Geneva (Switzerland) in February 2001 to vet the SPM line-by-line, proceeding to the next line only when all delegates agreed to do so.

While the science that underpins SPM was clear to its authors as their document was taken to the plenary for approval, the plenary is actually the final stage in this process of clarifying the message for policy makers. Discussions in the course of the plenary called attention to words and sentences that were perceived to be unclear by a delegate, and suggested changes were made as long as they were not inconsistent with the underlying science. By the conclusion of the meeting the Summary for Policymakers was approved in detail and the full report accepted by all delegations.

The Working Group Summary for Policy Makers is attached. It and related documents are available in pdf format at *www.usgcrp.gov/ipcc.*
The Summary for Policymakers.—Climate Change 2001: Impacts, Adaptation, and Vulnerability is being maintained in Committee files.

The CHAIRMAN. Thank you, Dr. McCarthy.
Dr. Lindzen.

STATEMENT OF DR. RICHARD S. LINDZEN, MASSACHUSETTS INSTITUTE OF TECHNOLOGY

Dr. LINDZEN. Thank you, Senator McCain, for the opportunity to appear before this Committee. I am a member of the NAS, and I also participated in the third assessment report as a lead author on chapter 7.

The CHAIRMAN. Chapter 7 was?

Dr. LINDZEN. The physics of climate. I come here usually designated as a skeptic. I am not sure what that means. I think in dealing with this, people are correct in saying that the science is complex, and I think the complexity is not only intrinsic, but has also resulted from the presentation of the issue, which in many ways has forced confusion and irrationality to dominate the discussion. It is presented as a multifaceted problem involving atmospheric composition, heat transfer, weather, temperature, ocean dynamics, hydrology, sea level, glaciology, ecology, and even epidemiology. All of these are subjects filled with uncertainty.

On the other hand, and I do not say any of my colleagues here today have done this, but you know that it is frequently said the science is settled. This is often said without any statement as to exactly what is meant by this, and what relevance it has to the forecast being made. The IPCC itself as a document is not particularly extreme, and I agree with my colleagues that it tends to present the science more or less as it is for better or for worse, but in the popular eye it is used as a mantra. It inevitably is used by people who wish to convince others that the science is settled, it is supported by thousands of scientists, and that this relieves them of the necessity to explain the science.

In point of fact, there are quite a few areas of agreement, and I think very few, if any of them, in any convincing way point to disaster, despite scenario creations of the type that Dr. McCarthy spoke of. For example, Dr. Ramaswamy mentioned things that are agreed upon, that the temperature has increased, that the CO_2 has increased, that CO_2 is more likely to cause warming than cooling, and I would add to that that man, like the butterfly, has some impact on climate.

What is frequently not realized is, the statements are as consistent with the statement that there will not be a problem as there will be a problem. They have very little substantive content, and yet they are perceived as having content.

In addition, we tend to raise issues that are different from warming, per se. To be sure, a few degrees of warming, or a degree does not particularly frighten the public. All of us who have had the extraordinary experience of day and night, winter and summer, have experienced far greater changes, so we go to what I think used to be called show-stoppers, increased weather extremes, increased variability, rising sea levels, and so on.

Now, I mention here a lot of things where there is widespread agreement on the science—that is hardly alarmist—but I will mention one specifically, and you can read some of the others in the testimony, and that has to do with increased weather extremes and disturbances. Here, the science for at least 40 years has noted that at least outside the tropics the main source of generating storms is the difference in temperature between the equator and pole.

Virtually all model predictions of global warming predict this will go down, and yet you have people always mentioning storminess. The cartoon I offer you emphasizes this. It should be going down, not up, by the basic physics.

When you see extremes in weather in any given season, it is because the wind changes from the north to south, and the extremes you see relate to how cold could a north wind be. That depends on how cold the Arctic is and how warm the tropics are. In other words, it depends on the pole-to-equator temperature difference. We are simultaneously hearing that these extremes will increase while the difference goes down. That is impossible, so in some sense alarmism has become a very important part of the issue, rather than the facts themselves.

The Kyoto agreement is also something that has been presented with utter confusion. I think there is widespread agreement that the Kyoto agreement, if adhered to, would have very little impact on climate. The estimates are, if you expected 4 degrees, you believed such models, you would knock it down to about 3.8.

In part, this is due to the fact that the Kyoto agreement applies only to the developed world, but even if extended to the whole world, harming the developing world rather severely, because that is at the heart of all claims that the developing world is more vulnerable. You are always more vulnerable if you are poor. You might knock it down from 4 to 3. In other words, if you expect severe warming, you will still have severe warming, so as a policy in itself, it seemed fairly ill-advised and ineffective.

Now, it has been mentioned that computer models are at the basis of much of our understanding, if you can call it that, and it is certainly at the basis of scenario-building. It has been mentioned, for example, that we are now surer that a large part of climate change is due to man. This is based on computer models. It is not a verification. You have to assume natural and internal variability generated by models is the same as it is in nature, and so we have circular projections.

This is part of our whole scenario system, where you no longer ask computer models to be correct. It is widely acknowledged that they are not. What you ask instead is that the projections be possible, and here the 1992 framework convention which we signed commits us to something called a precautionary principle, which now says all you have to do is suggest something is possible in order to need to act upon it.

I think that is a rather dangerous procedure, in any event, with such things as ill-defined possibilities and so on come to the IPCC, and we have heard from two people who participated very heavily in it, much more than I did, but there are a number of things with the IPCC that you should keep in mind.

First of all, even the summary, which does not adequately represent the text, is encouraging the media, the advocacy groups to misrepresent the summary. When the summary offers a range, however ill-advised, the media picked it up. When the summary says some part may be due to man, this is regarded as a smoking gun, even though it says no more than the advertising claim, savings up to 40 percent, which in fact permits them to overcharge you, so the use of language which conveys different meaning to layman and scientist is a serious issue.

The summary itself glosses over the text. There is no way you can conveniently summarize 1,000 pages in 13. With respect to the chapter on the physics, we went to considerable pains pointing out all the problems of the models. The summary simply concludes, understanding of climate processes and their incorporation in climate models have improved, including water vapor, sea ice dynamics, and ocean heat transport. That is not exactly the gist, and certainly with respect to clouds the statement was, all models completely fail to replicate clouds.

The statement that the IPCC represents hundreds of scientists does ignore the fact that hundreds of scientists are never asked. Each of them works on a few pages. The summary, the fact that the summary was worked on by a subset of about—you told me it was about 10 lead authors out of the hundreds ignores the fact that the summary's draft, which was prepared by these, itself was significantly changed in Shanghai.

I can testify that the preparation of the report itself was not only contentious, which is normal, but even after people with very different views had agreed, there was still pressure not to criticize models, to exaggerate the progress, and so on.

There is the final thing in the document that has such a technical importance on policy, that there are examples where the full text is modified long after the individual authors have signed off. I would say it is a very disturbing fact that the text was essentially complete last August, but is released, and as far as I know is still not released, long after the summary is released.

In any event, I do not think any of this is surprising. The IPCC was created in essence to support the negotiations, and without the negotiations, without the alarm, there would be no IPCC. It is not unusual that an organization has its own interests. The question I would like to go to and finish with is, where do we go from here?

I think it is extremely important in science policy, and that is where I have my own provincial interest, that we figure out how to support science without providing incentives for alarmism. I think you see here today an example that a field that promotes alarmism will get added attention. How do we assure scientists that they can find out that something is not alarming and still have support to figure out how nature works, instead of addressing it toward alarmism?

I think that is something that will definitely benefit future generations, the better understanding of nature, and this will far outweigh the benefits of any, if any, of ill-thought-out attempts to regulate nature in the absence of such understanding.

With respect to policy, I think the National Research Council in 1992 had a very lengthy report, Policy Implications of Greenhouse

Warming, and their main conclusion was, carry out only those actions which can be justified independently of any putative anthropogenic global warming, and here I would add that you not identify things with climate change unless they can be shown, unlike Kyoto, to have a significant impact on climate, otherwise it just becomes a coat hook.

Now, looking back at the picture on the first page of my testimony, you will notice they always picture emissions as being black. Remember that CO_2 is odorless and invisible, is essential to life, nontoxic, and is a normal product of breathing. When you portray it as black, you are already misleading the public.

Thank you.

[The prepared statement of Dr. Lindzen follows:]

PREPARED STATEMENT OF DR. RICHARD S. LINDZEN, MASSACHUSSETTS INSTITUTE OF TECHNOLOGY

I wish to thank Senator McCain and the Commerce Committee for the opportunity to clarify the nature of consensus and skepticism in the Climate Debate. I have been involved in climate and climate related research for over thirty years during which time I have held professorships at the University of Chicago, Harvard University and MIT. I am a member of the National Academy of Sciences, and the author or coauthor of over 200 papers and books. I have also been a participant in the proceedings of the IPCC (the United Nation's Intergovernmental Panel on Climate Change). The questions I wish to address are the following: What can we agree on and what are the implications of this agreement? What are the critical areas of disagreement? What is the origin of popular perceptions? I hope it will become clear that the designation, 'skeptic,' simply confuses an issue where popular perceptions are based in significant measure on misuse of language as well as misunderstanding of science. Indeed, the identification of some scientists as 'skeptics' permits others to appear 'mainstream' while denying views held by the so-called 'skeptics' even when these views represent the predominant views of the field.

Climate change is a complex issue where simplification tends to lead to confusion, and where understanding requires thought and effort. Judging from treatments of this issue in the press, the public has difficulty dealing with numerical magnitudes and focuses instead on signs (increasing v. decreasing); science places crucial emphasis on both signs and magnitudes. To quote the great 19th Century English scientist, Lord Kelvin, "When you can measure what you are speaking about and express it in numbers, you know something about it; but when you cannot measure it, when you cannot express it in numbers, your knowledge is of a meager and unsatisfactory kind."

As it turns out, much of what informed scientists agree upon is barely quantitative at all:
- that global mean temperature has probably increased over the past century,
- that CO_2 in the atmosphere has increased over the same period,
- that the added CO_2 is more likely to have caused global mean temperature to increase rather than decrease, and
- that man, like the butterfly, has some impact on climate.

Such statements have little relevance to policy, unless quantification shows significance.

The media and advocacy groups have, however, taken this agreement to mean that the same scientists must also agree that global warming "will lead to rising sea waters, droughts and agriculture disasters in the future if unchecked" (CNN). According to Deb Callahan, president of the League of Conservation Voters, "Science clearly shows that we are experiencing devastating impacts because of carbon dioxide pollution." (Carbon dioxide, as a 'pollutant' is rather singular in that it is a natural product of respiration, non-toxic, and essential for life.) The accompanying cartoon suggests implications for severe weather, the ecosystem, and presumably plague, floods and droughts (as well as the profound politicization of the issue). Scientists who do not agree with the catastrophe scenarios are assumed to disagree with the basic statements. This is not only untrue, but absurdly stupid.

Indeed, the whole issue of consensus and skeptics is a bit of a red herring. If, as the news media regularly report, global warming is the increase in temperature caused by man's emissions of CO_2 that will give rise to rising sea levels, floods, droughts, weather extremes of all sorts, plagues, species elimination, and so on, then it is safe to say that global warming consists in so many aspects, that widespread agreement on all of them would be suspect *ab initio*. If it truly existed, it would be evidence of a thoroughly debased field. In truth, neither the full text of the IPCC documents nor even the summaries claim any such agreement. Those who insist that the science is settled should be required to state exactly what science they feel is settled. In all likelihood, it will turn out to be something trivial and without policy implications except to those who bizarrely subscribe to the so-called precautionary principle—a matter I will return to later. (Ian Bowles, former senior science advisor on environmental issues at the NSC, published such a remark on 22 April in the Boston Globe: "the basic link between carbon emissions, accumulation of greenhouse gases in the atmosphere, and the phenomenon of climate change is not seriously disputed in the scientific community." I think it is fair to say that statements concerning matters of such complexity that are not disputed are also likely to be lacking in policy relevant content. However, some policymakers apparently think otherwise in a cultural split that may be worthy of the late C.P. Snow's attention.)

The thought that there might be a central question, whose resolution would settle matters, is, of course, inviting, and there might, in fact, be some basis for optimism. While determining whether temperature has increased or not is *not* such a question, the determination of climate sensitivity might be. Rather little serious attention has been given to this matter (though I will mention some in the course of this testimony). However, even ignoring this central question, there actually is much that can be learned simply by sticking to matters where there is widespread agreement. For example, there is widespread agreement

- that CO_2 levels have increased from about 280ppm to 360ppm over the past century, and, that combined with increases in other greenhouse gases, this brings us about half way to the radiative forcing associated with a doubling of CO_2 without any evidence of enhanced human misery.
- that the increase in global mean temperature over the past century is about 1F which is smaller than the normal interannual variability for smaller regions like North America and Europe, and comparable to the interannual variability for the globe. Which is to say that temperature is always changing, which is why it has proven so difficult to demonstrate human agency.
- that doubling CO_2 *alone* will only lead to about a 2F increase in global mean temperature. Predictions of greater warming due to doubling CO_2 are based on positive feedbacks from poorly handled water vapor and clouds (the atmosphere's main greenhouse substances) in current computer models. Such positive feedbacks have neither empirical nor theoretical foundations. Their existence, however, suggests a poorly designed earth which responds to perturbations by making things worse.
- that the most important energy source for extratropical storms is the temperature difference between the tropics and the poles which is predicted by computer models to decrease with global warming. This also implies reduced temperature variation associated with weather since such variations result from air moving from one latitude to another. Consistent with this, even the IPCC Policymakers Summary notes that no significant trends have been identified in tropical or extratropical storm intensity and frequence. Nor have trends been found in tornados, hail events or thunder days.
- that warming is likely to be concentrated in winters and at night. This is an empirical result based on data from the past century. It represents what is on the whole a beneficial pattern.
- that temperature increases observed thus far are less than what models have suggested should have occurred even if they were totally due to increasing greenhouse emissions. The invocation of very uncertain (and unmeasured) aerosol effects is frequently used to disguise this. Such an invocation makes it impossible to check models. Rather, one is reduced to the claim that it is *possible* that models are correct.
- that claims that man has contributed any of the observed warming (ie attribution) are based on the assumption that models correctly predict natural variability. Such claims, therefore, do not constitute independent verifications of models. Note that natural variability does not require any *external* forcing—natural or anthropogenic.
- that large computer climate models are unable to even simulate major features of past climate such as the 100 thousand year cycles of ice ages that have dominated climate for the past 700 thousand years, and the very warm climates of the Miocene, Eocene, and Cretaceous. Neither do they do well at accounting for shorter period and less dramatic phenomena like El Niños, quasi-biennial oscillations, or intraseasonal oscillations—all of which are well documented in the data, and important contributors to natural variability.

- that major past climate changes were either uncorrelated with changes in CO_2 or were characterized by temperature changes which preceded changes in CO_2 by 100's to thousands of years.
- that increases in temperature on the order of 1F are not catastrophic and may be beneficial.
- that Kyoto, fully implemented, will have little detectable impact on climate regardless of what one expects for warming. This is partly due to the fact that Kyoto will apply only to developed nations. However, if one expected large global warming, even the extension of Kyoto to developing nations would still leave one with large warming.

None of the above points to catastrophic consequences from increasing CO_2. Most point towards, and all are consistent with minimal impacts. Moreover, the last item provides a definitive disconnect between Kyoto and science. Should a catastrophic scenario prove correct, Kyoto will not prevent it. *If we view Kyoto as an insurance policy, it is a policy where the premium appears to exceed the potential damages, and where the coverage extends to only a small fraction of the potential damages.* Does anyone really want this? I suspect not. Given the rejection of the extensive US concessions at the Hague, it would appear that the Europeans do not want the treaty, but would prefer that the US take the blame for ending the foolishness. As a practical matter, a large part of the response to any climate change, natural or anthropogenic, will be adaptation, and that adaptation is best served by wealth.

Our own research suggests the presence of a major negative feedback involving clouds and water vapor, where models have completely failed to simulate observations (to the point of getting the sign wrong for crucial dependences). If we are right, then models are greatly exaggerating sensitivity to increasing CO_2. Even if we are not right (which is always possible in science; for example, IPCC estimates of warming trends for the past twenty years were almost immediately acknowledged to be wrong—so too were claims for arctic ice thinning), the failure of models to simulate observations makes it even less likely that models are a reliable tool for predicting climate.

This brings one to what is probably the major point of disagreement:

Can one trust computer climate models to correctly predict the response to increasing CO_2?

As the accompanying cartoon suggests, our experience with weather forecasts is not particularly encouraging though it may be argued that the prediction of gross climate changes is not as demanding as predicting the detailed weather. Even here, the situation is nuanced. From the perspective of the *precautionary principle*, it suffices to believe that the existence of a computer prediction of an adverse situation means that such an outcome is *possible* rather than *correct* in order to take 'action.' The burden of proof has shifted to proving that the computer prediction is wrong. Such an approach effectively deprives society of science's capacity to solve problems and answer questions. Unfortunately, the incentive structure in today's scientific enterprise contributes to this impasse. *Scientists associate public recognition of the relevance of their subject with support, and relevance has come to be identified with alarming the public.* It is only human for scientists to wish for support and recognition, and the broad agreement among scientists that climate change is a serious issue must be viewed from this human perspective. Indeed, *public perceptions have significantly influenced the science itself*. Meteorologists, oceanographers, hydrologists and others at MIT have all been redesignated climate scientists—indicating the degree to which scientists have hitched their futures to this issue.

That said, it has become common to deal with the science by referring to the IPCC 'scientific consensus.' Claiming the agreement of thousands of scientists is certainly easier than trying to understand the issue or to respond to scientific questions; it also effectively intimidates most citizens. However, the *invocation of the IPCC is more a mantra than a proper reflection on that flawed document*. The following points should be kept in mind. (Note that almost all reading and coverage of the IPCC is restricted to the highly publicized Summaries for Policymakers which are written by representatives from governments, NGO's and business; the full reports, written by participating scientists, are largely ignored.) In what follows, I will largely restrict myself to the report of Working Group I (on the science). Working Groups II and III dealt with impacts and responses.

- *The media reports rarely reflect what is actually in the Summary.* The media generally replace the IPCC range of 'possible' temperature increases with 'as much as' the maximum—despite the highly unlikely nature of the maximum. The range, itself, assumes, unjustifiably, that at least some of the computer models must be correct. However, there is evidence that even the bottom of the range is an overestimate. (A recent study at MIT found that the likelihood of actual change being smaller than the IPCC lower bound was 17 times more likely than that the upper range would even be reached, and even this study assumed natural variability to be what computer models predicted, thus exaggerating the role of anthropogenic forcing.) The media report storminess as a consequence despite the admission in the summary of no such observed relation. To be sure, the summary still claims that such a relation may emerge—despite the fact that the underlying physics suggests the opposite. The media's emphasis on increased storminess, rising sea levels, etc. is based not on any science, but rather on the fact that such features have more graphic impact than the rather small increases in temperature. People who have experienced day and night and winter and summer have experienced far greater changes in temperature, and retirement to the sun belt rather than the Northwest Territory represents an overt preference for warmth.

- *The summary does not reflect the full document (which still has not been released although it was basically completed last August).* For example, I worked on Chapter 7, Physical Processes. This chapter dealt with the nature of the basic processes which determine the response of climate, and found numerous problems with model treatments—including those of clouds and water vapor. The chapter was summarized with the following sentence: "Understanding of climate processes and their incorporation in climate models have improved, including water vapour, sea-ice dynamics, and ocean heat transport."
- *The vast majority of participants played no role in preparing the summary, and were not asked for agreement.*
- *The draft of the Policymakers Summary was significantly modified at Shanghai.* The IPCC, in response to the fact that the Policymakers Summary was not prepared by participating scientists, claimed that the draft of the Summary was prepared by a (selected) subset of the 14 coordinating lead authors. However, the final version of the summary differed significantly from the draft. For example the draft concluded the following concerning attribution:

From the body of evidence since IPCC (1996), we conclude that there has been a discernible human influence on global climate. Studies are beginning to separate the contributions to observed climate change attributable to individual external influences, both anthropogenic and natural. This work suggests that anthropogenic greenhouse gases are a substantial contributor to the observed warming, especially over the past 30 years. However, the accuracy of these estimates continues to be limited by uncertainties in estimates of internal variability, natural and anthropogenic forcing, and the climate response to external forcing.

The version that emerged from Shanghai concludes instead:

In the light of new evidence and taking into account the remaining uncertainties, most of the observed warming over the last 50 years is likely to have been due to the increase in greenhouse gas concentrations.

In point of fact, there may not have been any significant warming in the last 60 years. Moreover, such warming as may have occurred was associated with jumps that are inconsistent with greenhouse warming.

- *The preparation of the report, itself, was subject to pressure.* There were usually several people working on every few pages. Naturally there were disagreements, but these were usually hammered out in a civilized manner. However, throughout the drafting sessions, IPCC 'coordinators' would go around insisting that criticism of models be toned down, and that 'motherhood' statements be inserted to the effect that models might still be correct despite the cited faults. Refusals were occasionally met with ad hominem attacks. I personally witnessed coauthors forced to assert their 'green' credentials in defense of their statements.

None of the above should be surprising. The IPCC was created to support the negotiations concerning CO_2 emission reductions. Although the press frequently refers to the hundreds and even thousands of participants as the world's leading climate scientists, such a claim is misleading on several grounds. First, climate science, itself, has traditionally been a scientific backwater. There is little question that the best science students traditionally went into physics, math and, more recently, computer science. Thus, speaking of 'thousands' of the world's leading climate scientists is not especially meaningful. Even within climate science, most of the top researchers (at least in the US) avoid the IPCC because it is extremely time consuming and non-productive. Somewhat ashamedly I must admit to being the only active participant in my department. None of this matters a great deal to the IPCC. As a UN activity, it is far more important to have participants from a hundred countries—many of which have almost no active efforts in climate research. For most of these participants, involvement with the IPCC gains them prestige beyond what would normally be available, and these, not surprisingly, are likely to be particularly supportive of the IPCC. Finally, judging from the Citation Index, the leaders of the IPCC process like Sir John Houghton, Dr. Robert Watson, and Prof. Bert Bolin have never been major contributors to basic climate research. They are, however, enthusiasts for the negotiating process without which there would be no IPCC, which is to say that the IPCC represents an interest in its own right. Of course, this hardly distinguishes the IPCC from other organizations.

The question of where do we go from here is an obvious and important one. From my provincial perspective, an important priority should be given to figuring out how to support and encourage science (and basic science underlying climate in particular) while removing incentives to promote alarmism. The benefits of leaving future generations a better understanding of nature would far outweigh the benefits (if any) of ill thought out attempts to regulate nature in the absence of such understanding. With respect to any policy, the advice given in the 1992 report of the NRC, *Policy Implications of Greenhouse Warming*, remains relevant: carry out only those actions which can be justified independently of any putative anthropogenic global warming. Here, I would urge that even such actions not be identified with climate unless they can be shown to significantly impact the radiative forcing of climate. On neither ground—independent justification or climatic relevance—is Kyoto appropriate.

The CHAIRMAN. Thank you.
Dr. Sathaye.

STATEMENT OF DR. JAYANT A. SATHAYE, SENIOR SCIENTIST, LAWRENCE BERKELEY NATIONAL LABORATORY, UNIVERSITY OF CALIFORNIA

Dr. SATHAYE. Thank you, Mr. Chairman, for inviting me.

I am a senior scientist at the Lawrence Berkeley National Laboratory operated by the University of California. I have worked as a Coordinating Lead Author of one of the chapters, the Third Assessment Report of the Third Working Group, and I have also served in a similar capacity on other IPCC reports over the last 7 years or so.

The main points that I want to make today deal with two segments, two time periods, one dealing with the reduction of near-term annual greenhouse gas emissions, and the second dealing with the long-term stabilization of climate change. With regards to the near-term annual greenhouse gas emissions, the IPCC concluded that there were many technologies already available in the marketplace, which have the potential to reduce global greenhouse gas emissions from 2010 to 2020 to levels below those of 2000 and this is something you pointed out, Mr. Chairman in your statement. About half of the reduction potential can be achieved with direct benefits, exceeding the direct cost, and the other half at a net direct cost of $100 per ton of carbon equivalent.

Now, this may seem somewhat optimistic and, indeed, if you tried to deploy these technologies in the marketplace you would encounter a number of different barriers, and these barriers include things like subsidized prices, world capital markets, lack of access to information and so forth, and we have a whole chapter in the IPCC that deals with just these issues. The implications of these barriers are that it will take time in order to implement the technologies that are available to us, and they will add to the cost of implementing these technologies as well.

Let me go on to talk about another aspect of the near-term cost, and this deals with a whole array of studies that have been done about the cost to various industrial economies if they were to meet the levels of emissions constraints specified in the Kyoto Protocol. The studies showed that the cost to the U.S. economy would range between 0.4 to 2 percent of the U.S. GDP in the year 2010.

Now, there are a number of ways the cost could be reduced and this, too, has been referred to earlier. One of the more important ways this cost could be reduced is through full emissions trading across industrialized countries. Just by that approach alone, these costs could be reduced by 50 percent, and we have experience with this, with sulphur dioxide trading within the United States and, indeed, that was a very effective approach to reducing sulphur dioxide emissions from power plants in the United States. But the cost can be further reduced if you pursue carbon dioxide projects in developing countries and also include land use change and forestry options in addition to other technologies.

Now, Dr. Lindzen just mentioned this question about pursuing approaches that also address other benefits that you might derive from mitigation actions and so if you pursue options that also reduce local pollutants, this could have a double or joint benefit whereby you achieve reductions in local pollutants as well as reduction of greenhouse gases.

Let me now turn to the second topic, which has to do with the stabilization of long-term atmospheric greenhouse gas concentrations. What the IPCC report concludes is that in this case as well, the technological options that we need in order to stabilize climate at levels of 450 parts per million, for instance, which is about 20 percent over the levels in the year 2000, those technological options are known as well, so we are not looking for exotic technologies in order to stabilize climate change if we decide that that is what we want to do over the long term.

In terms of the cost of achieving such stabilization, it will depend upon what stabilization level we pick as well as the emissions pathway to that stabilization level, and least-cost studies show that the lower the stabilization level, the more it will reach that level. The lower stabilization level means you begin earlier to decrease emissions as well.

Stabilization will require the participation of all countries. All IPCC emission scenarios show one trend consistently, that you cannot stabilize unless all countries participate in this process. The emission scenarios also indicate that conventional oil and gas resources will be severely depleted by mid-century or earlier. This is true for all emission scenarios that IPCC has looked at, and what this implies is that there will be an opportunity, or opportunities to shift or make a transition to less-carbon-intensive energy sources and technologies as the conventional oil and gas resources are depleted.

Finally, Mr. Chairman, in order to achieve these kinds of technological breakthroughs, investments in energy R&D, the transfer existing technologies is going to play a critical role not just in the United States but worldwide if climate is to be stabilized.

Let me also make a couple of remarks about the IPCC process. I think all of us here have participated in that process to some degree, and perhaps one thing that is probably worth clearing up is that the IPCC is engaged in reviews of studies, research studies that have already been done.

There is no new research being done within the IPCC work, and it is completely compatible with national governments, or national institutions carrying out research as mandated, or as required by governments on their own, and I think this is important to remember, that if there was no research done, there would be nothing for the IPCC to review.

The second point about the IPCC is that we are providing information to negotiators, but we also are providing summarized information to all concerned. It is not just to the government, the negotiators. It goes to academics, it goes to students, and can be shared with everyone.

Lastly, you can do studies and nobody ever reads them, they go on bookshelves, and you can do studies in which the governments participate actively. In the IPCC process there is, indeed, some give-and-take, but we make sure that the content of the IPCC report remains in the summaries and, given that, I think there is a value to that process of consensus-building and pulling together this information in a summarized form.

Let me conclude with that, and thank you again, Mr. Chairman for inviting me.

[The prepared statement of Dr. Sathaye follows:]

PREPARED STATEMENT OF DR. JAYANT A. SATHAYE[1], SENIOR SCIENTIST, LAWRENCE BERKELEY NATIONAL LABORATORY, UNIVERSITY OF CALIFORNIA

SUMMARY

The IPCC WG III review of studies on climate change mitigation describes the potential and costs of technologies, practices, and policies to (1) reduce near-term annual greenhouse gas (GHG) emissions, and (2) stabilize atmospheric GHG concentrations over the long-term.

Reduction of Near-term Annual GHG Emissions:

1. Significant unanticipated technical progress relevant to greenhouse gas reductions has been achieved since the IPCC released its Second Assessment Report in 1996.

2. Technologies such as efficient hybrid engine cars, fuel cells, underground carbon dioxide storage, and many others have the potential to reduce global GHG emissions in 2010—2020 to below 2000 levels.

3. In the absence of barriers, studies suggest that about half of the above emissions reduction potential can be achieved with direct benefits exceeding direct costs, and the other half at a net direct cost of up to US $ 100/t Ceq (at 1998 prices). Overcoming barriers such as subsidized prices, lack of access to information and financing, and ill defined property rights will incur additional costs, which in some cases may be substantial.

4. National responses can be more effective if deployed as a portfolio of policy instruments to reduce greenhouse gas emissions.

5. About a dozen studies based on models of the global economy estimate that costs to the US economy of meeting GHG emissions levels noted in the Kyoto Protocol vary from 0.4–2.0% of 2010 GDP.

6. Assuming full GHG emissions trading both within and across industrialized countries, these studies show that costs can be reduced to less than half the above values.

7. Costs may be further reduced through implementation of carbon offset projects in developing countries, and land use, land-use change and forestry (LULUCF) activities, mitigation options that also reduce local pollutants, and revenue neutral carbon taxes.

Stabilization of Long-term (2100+) Atmospheric GHG Concentrations:

8. Widespread use of known technological options could achieve a broad range of atmospheric carbon dioxide stabilization levels such as 550, 450 ppmv or below (compared to 368 ppmv in 2000) over the next 100 years or more, if the type of barriers noted in item 3 above could be overcome.

9. The cost of achieving stabilization will depend on the emissions pathway and the targeted stabilization level. Least-cost studies show that decreasing the stabilization target makes annual emissions peak earlier and at lower levels before be-

---

[1] The remarks in this statement represent my personal views, and not necessarily those of the Lawrence Berkeley National Laboratory or the University of California.

ginning a gradual decline, and vice versa. Estimated costs of stabilizing carbon dioxide concentrations increase steeply as the level declines below 550 ppmv.

10. Stabilization will require the participation of all countries. Two-thirds of IPCC Post-SRES scenarios show that annual GHG emissions per capita from industrialized countries decline to levels below those of developing countries by 2050.

11. IPCC emissions scenarios indicate a severe depletion of conventional oil and gas resources by mid-century or earlier. This offers an opportunity for a transition to less-carbon-intensive energy sources and technologies.

12. Investment in energy R&D, the transfer and adoption of existing technology, and technological and social innovation will be required to foster the penetration of these energy sources and improved technologies.

RESULTS AND CONCLUSIONS

Mr. Chairman, thank you for inviting me to speak about the findings of the Working Group (WG) III on *Climate Change 2001: Mitigation* of the Intergovernmental Panel on Climate Change (IPCC). I served as a Coordinating Lead Author of the Chapter on Barriers, Opportunities, and Market Potential of Technologies and Practices of the WG III report, and an author of the Synthesis Report, and have participated in the discussions and writing of their Summaries for Policy Makers (SPM). My remarks today are based largely on the SPM findings and the contents of the underlying report. In this statement, I have focused on the near- and long-term potential for, and costs and benefits of, reducing reenhouse gas emissions.

1. There are many low cost technological options to reduce near-term emissions, but barriers to their deployment exist.

Significant technical progress relevant to the potential for greenhouse gas emission reductions has been made since 1995 and has been faster than anticipated. Net emissions reductions could be achieved through, inter-alia, improved production and use of energy, shift to low- or no-carbon technologies, carbon removal and storage, and improved land-use, land-use change and forestry (LULUCF) practices. Relevant advances are taking place in a wide range of technologies at different stages of development, ranging from the market introduction of efficient hybrid engine cars to the advancement of fuel cell technology, and the demonstration of underground carbon dioxide storage.

The successful implementation of greenhouse gas mitigation options would need to overcome many technical, economic, political, cultural, social, behavioral and/or institutional barriers which prevent the full exploitation of the technological, economic and social opportunities of these mitigation options (Figure 1). The potential mitigation opportunities and types of barriers vary by region and sector, and over time. In the industrialized countries, future opportunities lie primarily in removing social and behavioral barriers, in countries with economies in transition, in price rationalization; and in developing countries, in price rationalization, increased access to data and information, availability of advanced technologies, financial resources, and training and capacity building. Most countries could benefit from innovative financing and institutional reform and removing barriers to trade.

National responses to climate change can be more effective if deployed as a portfolio of policy instruments to limit or reduce greenhouse gas emissions. The portfolio may include—according to national circumstances- emissions/carbon/energy taxes, tradable or non-tradable permits, subsidies, deposit/refund systems, technology or performance standards, product bans, voluntary agreements, government spending and investment, and support for research and development.

Annual global emissions reductions of 1.9–2.6 GtCeq, and 3.6—5.0 GtCeq per year could be achieved by 2010 and 2020 respectively, with half of these reductions being realized with direct benefits exceeding direct costs, and the other half at a net direct cost of up to US$100/tCeq (at 1998 prices). Depending on the emissions scenario this could allow global emissions to be reduced below 2000 levels in 2010–2020 (Table 1). These cost estimates are derived using discount rates in the range of 5 to 12 percent, consistent with public sector discount rates, but lower than private internal rates of return, thus affecting the rate of adoption of these technologies by private entities. Realising these reductions involves, among other things, additional implementation costs, which in some cases may be substantial, the possible need for supporting policies, increased research and development, and effective technology transfer.

2. Based on models of the global economy the cost estimates of meeting GHG emissions levels noted in the Kyoto Protocol vary considerably both within and across regions.

Models show that the Kyoto mechanisms can reduce costs to Annex II[2] countries. Global modeling studies show national marginal costs to meet the Kyoto emissions levels range from about US$20/tC up to US$600/tC without trading, and from about US$15/tC up to US$150/tC with Annex B[3] trading. Figure 2 shows the range of GDP losses estimated in these studies in 2010. The cost reductions and GDP losses from these mechanisms may depend on the details of implementation, including the compatibility of domestic and international mechanisms, constraints, and transaction costs. These costs can be further reduced through use of the Clean Development Mechanism, LULUCF activities, by including the non-carbon dioxide gases, identifying and implementing options that produce ancillary benefits, and identifying double dividend opportunities, e.g., carbon taxes or auctioned permits may be used to finance reductions in existing distortionary taxes, reducing the economic cost of achieving greenhouse gas reductions.

Emission constraints in Annex I[4] countries have well established, albeit varied "spill over" effects on non-Annex I countries, including:

Oil-exporting, non-Annex I countries: The study reporting the lowest costs, reported reductions in projected GDP of 0.2% with no emissions trading, and less than 0.05% with Annex B emissions trading in 2010. The study reporting the highest costs shows reductions of projected oil revenues of 25% with no emissions trading, and 13% with Annex B emissions trading in 2010.

Other non-Annex I countries may be adversely affected by reductions in demand for their exports to OECD nations and by the price increase of those carbon-intensive and other products they continue to import, but may benefit from the reduction in fuel prices, increased exports of carbon-intensive products and the transfer of environmentally sound technologies and know how.

3. Technology development and diffusion are an important component of cost-effective stabilization.

Transfer of existing technologies and the development and transfer of new technologies could play a critical role in reducing the cost of stabilizing greenhouse gas concentrations. Transfer of technologies between countries and regions could widen the choice of options at the regional level and economies of scale and learning will lower the costs of their adoption. Governments through sound economic policy, and regulatory frameworks, transparency and political stability could create an enabling environment for private and public sector technology transfers and adequate human and organizational capacity is essential at every stage to increase the flow, and improve the quality, of technologies. In addition, networking among private and public stakeholders, and focusing on products and techniques with multiple ancillary benefits, that meet or adapt to local needs and priorities, is essential for most effective technology transfers.

IPCC emissions scenarios indicate that conventional oil and gas resources will be mostly used up by mid-century irrespective of actions to address climate change (Figure 3). This will necessitate a different pattern of energy resource development and an increase in energy R&D with the goal of accelerating the development and deployment of advanced energy technologies. Given that the carbon in proven conventional oil and gas reserves, or in conventional oil resources, is limited, this may imply a change in the energy mix and the introduction of new sources of energy during the 21st century. If so, the choice of energy mix and associated investment will determine whether, and if so, at what level and cost, greenhouse concentrations can be stabilized. Opportunities that exist in the near term are the fruits of past investments in energy R&D; therefore, further investments in energy R&D will be required to maintain the flow of improved energy technologies throughout the 21st century.

Technological and social innovation could raise the social and economic potential of mitigation options beyond that of current markets. In the longer term, such innovations may shift preferences and cultural norms towards lower-emitting and sustainable behaviors.

4. Both the *pathway to stabilization* of atmospheric GHG concentrations and the *stabilization target* itself are key determinants of mitigation costs

Stabilization levels depend more on cumulative rather than year-by-year emissions. A gradual near-term transition away from the world's present energy system towards a less carbon-emitting economy minimizes costs associated with premature

---

[2] Annex II: Countries listed in the Annex II of the UN Framework Convention on Climate Change. Annex II list includes the United States and 23 other original members of the Organization for Economic Cooperation and Development (OECD), plus the European Union.

[3] Annex B: Annex I countries that are listed in the Kyoto Protocol to take on commitments to limit their emissions.

[4] Annex I: Annex II countries plus the countries designated as Economies in Transition.

retirement of existing capital stock and provides time for technology development, and avoids premature lock-in to early versions of rapidly developing low-emission technology, where-as more rapid near-term action would decrease environmental and human risks associated with projected changes in climate and may stimulate more rapid deployment of existing low-emission technologies and provide strong near-term incentives to future technological changes.

Studies show that the costs of stabilizing carbon dioxide concentrations in the atmosphere increase as the stabilization level declines (Figure 4). While there is a moderate increase in the costs when passing from a 750 ppm to a 550 ppm concentration stabilization level, there is a larger increase in costs passing from 550 ppm to 450 ppm unless the emissions in the baseline scenario are very low. However, these studies did not incorporate carbon sequestration, non-carbon dioxide gases and did not examine the possible effect of more ambitious targets on induced technological change.

Countries and regions will have to choose their own path to a low emissions future, where decision-making is essentially a sequential process under uncertainty. Most model results indicate that known technological options could achieve a broad range of atmospheric carbon dioxide stabilization levels, such as 550 ppm or 450 ppm and below over the next 100 years or more, but implementation would require associated socio-economic and institutional changes. However, no single sector or technology option could provide all of the emissions reductions needed. A prudent risk management strategy requires a careful consideration of the economic and environmental consequences, their likelihood and society's attitude toward risk.

Stabilization of atmospheric GHG levels will require the participation of all countries in the long term. Two-thirds of IPCC Post-SRES scenarios show that annual GHG emissions per capita from industrialized countries decline to levels below those of developing countries by 2050.

Figure 1: Penetration of Environmentally Sound Technologies (including Practices): A Conceptual Framework

Various barriers prevent the different potentials from being realized. Opportunities exist to overcome barriers through innovative projects, programs and financing arrangements. An action can address more than one barrier. Actions may be pursued to address barriers at all levels simultaneously. Their implementation may require public policies, measures and instruments. The socioeconomic potential may lie anywhere in the space between the economic and technological potential.

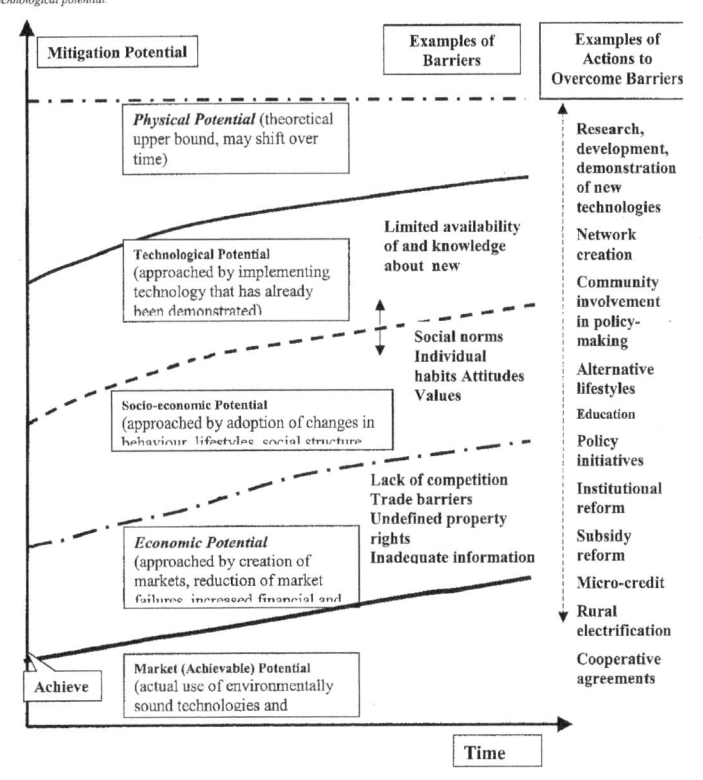

Mitigation Potential	Examples of Barriers	Examples of Actions to Overcome Barriers
Physical Potential (theoretical upper bound, may shift over time)		Research, development, demonstration of new technologies
Technological Potential (approached by implementing technology that has already been demonstrated)	Limited availability of and knowledge about new	Network creation
	Social norms Individual habits Attitudes Values	Community involvement in policy-making
Socio-economic Potential (approached by adoption of changes in behaviour, lifestyles, social structure		Alternative lifestyles
		Education
	Lack of competition Trade barriers Undefined property rights Inadequate information	Policy initiatives
Economic Potential (approached by creation of markets, reduction of market failures, increased financial and		Institutional reform
		Subsidy reform
		Micro-credit
		Rural electrification
Achieve — *Market (Achievable) Potential* (actual use of environmentally sound technologies and		Cooperative agreements

Time

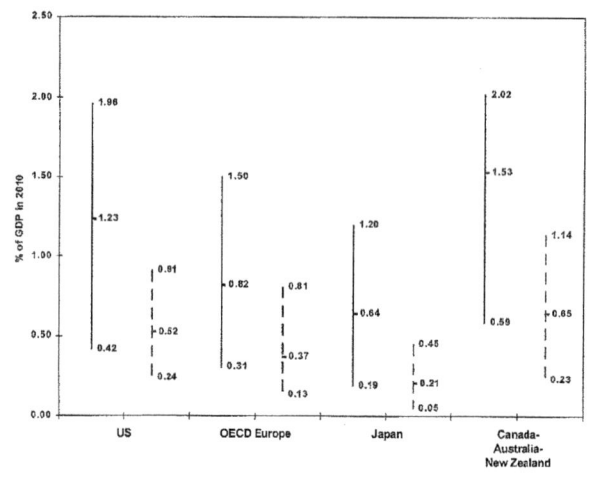

Figure 2. Global model projections of GDP losses in Annex II in 2010. The projections are from the Energy Modeling Forum study cited in WGIII Section 8.3.1.1. The global models used in that study dissagregate the world into regions. The projections reported in the figure are for four regions, which constitute Annex II. The models examined two scenarios. In the first, each region must make the prescribed reduction in the absence of international trade in carbon emissions rights (solid lines). In the second, full Annex B trading is permitted (dashed lines). For each region, the maximum, minimum, and average of the model projections are shown.

Figure 3. Carbon in oil, gas and coal reserves and resources compared with historic fossil fuel carbon emissions 1860-1998, and with cumulative carbon emissions from a range of SRES scenarios and TAR stabilization scenarios up until 2100. Data for reserves and resources are shown in the left hand columns (Section 3.8.1). Unconventional oil and gas includes tar sands, shale oil, other heavy oil, coal bed methane, deep geopressured gas, gas in acquifers, etc. Gas hydrates (clathrates) that amount to an estimated 12,000 GtC are not shown. The scenario columns show both SRES reference scenarios as well as scenarios which lead to stabilization of CO_2 concentrations at a range of levels. Note that if by 2100 cumulative emissions associated with SRES scenarios are equal to or smaller than those for stabilization scenarios, this does not imply that these scenarios equally lead to stabilization.

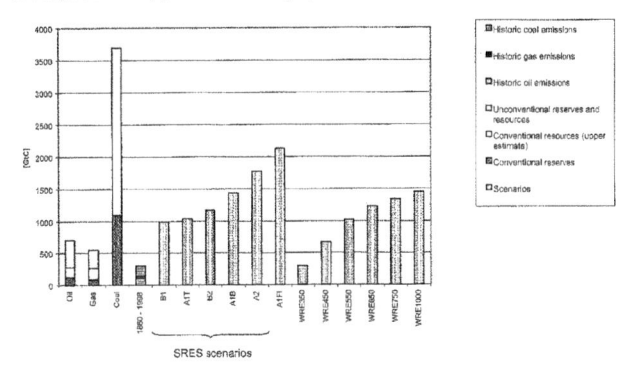

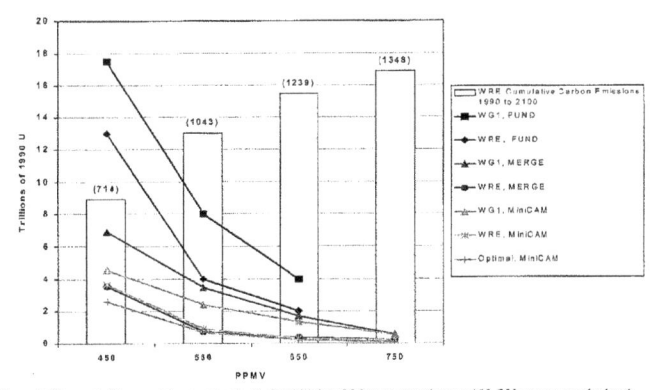

Figure 4. The costs (discounted present value) of stabilizing CO2 concentrations at 450-750ppmv are calculated using three global models. In each instance, costs were calculated based on two emission pathways for achieving the prescribed target: WGI or S and WRE. The MiniCam model was also used to identify the least-cost emissions pathway. The bar chart shows cumulative carbon emissions between 1990 and 2100.

Table 1. Estimates of potential global greenhouse gas emission reductions in 2010 and in 2020

Sector		Historic emissions in 1990 [MtC_eq/yr]	Historic C_eq. annual growth rate in 1990-1995 [%]	Potential emission reductions in 2010 [MtC_eq/yr]	Potential emission reductions in 2020 [MtC_eq/yr]	Net direct costs per tonne of carbon avoided
Buildings[a]	CO_2 only	1650	1.0	700-750	1000-1100	Most reductions are available at negative net direct costs.
Transport	CO_2 only	1080	2.4	100-300	300-700	Most studies indicate net direct costs less than $25/tC but two suggest net direct costs will exceed $50/tC.
Industry -energy efficiency: -material efficiency:	CO_2 only	2300	0.4	300-500 ~200	700-900 ~600	More than half available at net negative direct costs. Costs are uncertain.
Industry	Non-CO_2 gases	170		~100	~100	N_2O emissions reduction costs are $0-$10/tC_eq.
Agriculture[b]	CO_2 only Non-CO_2 gases	210 1250-2800	n.a	150-300	350-750	Most reductions will cost between $0-100/tC_eq with limited opportunities for negative net direct cost options
Waste[b]	CH_4 only	240	1.0	~200	~200	About 75% of the savings as methane recovery from landfills at net negative direct cost; 25% at a cost of $20/tC_eq.
Montreal Protocol replacement applications	Non-CO_2 gases	0	n.a.	~100	n.a.	About half of reductions due to difference in study baseline and SRES baseline values. Remaining half of the reductions available at net direct costs below $200/tC_eq.
Energy supply and conversion[c]	CO_2 only	(1620)	1.5	50-150	350-700	Limited net negative direct cost options exist; many options are available for less than $100/tCeq.
Total		6,900-8,400[d]		1,900-2,600[e]	3,600-5,050[e]	

[a] Buildings include appliances, buildings, and the building shell.
[b] The range for agriculture is mainly caused by large uncertainties about CH_4, N_2O and soil related emissions of CO_2. Waste is dominated by methane landfill and the other sectors could be estimated with more precision as they are dominated by fossil CO_2.
[c] Included in sector values above. Reductions include electricity generation options only (fuel switching to gas/nuclear, CO_2 capture and storage, improved power station efficiencies, and renewables).
[d] Total includes all sectors reviewed in Chapter 3 for all six gases. It excludes non-energy related sources of CO_2 (cement production, 160MtC; gas flaring, 60MtC; and land use change, 600-1400MtC) and energy used for conversion of fuels in the end-use sector totals (630MtC). Note that forestry emissions and their carbon sink mitigation options are not included.
[e] The baseline SRES scenarios (for six gases included in the Kyoto Protocol) project a range of emissions of 11,500-14,000 MtC_eq for 2010 and of 12,000-16,000MtC_eq for 2020. The emissions reduction estimates are most compatible with baseline emissions trends in the SRES-B2 scenario. The potential reductions take into account regular turn-

Table 1 (Continued). Estimates of potential global greenhouse gas emission reductions in 2010 and in 2020

Sector	Historic emissions in 1990 [MtC_eq/yr]	Historic C_eq annual growth rate in 1990-1995 [%]	Potential emission reductions in 2010 [MtC_eq/yr]	Potential emission reductions in 2020 [MtC_eq/yr]	Comments
Land Use, Land-use Change and Forestry					
Afforestation/Reforestation [F] (AR)			197-584		Includes carbon in above and below-ground biomass. Excludes carbon in soils and in dead organic matter.
Reducing Deforestation [F] (D)			1788		Potential for reducing deforestation is very uncertain for the tropics and could be in error by as much as +−50%.
Improved management within a land use [g] (IM)			570		Assumed to be the best available suite of management practices for each land use and climatic zone.
Land-use change [g] (LC)			435		
Total AR, IM, and LC			1202-1589		
D			1788		

over of capital stock. They are not limited to cost-effective options, but exclude options with costs above US$100/tC_eq (except for Montreal Protocol gases) or options that will not be adopted through the use of generally accepted policies.

F Source: Table 3, SPM, SR LULUCF. Based on IPCC definitional scenario. Information is not available for other definitional scenarios. Potential refers to the estimated range of accounted average stock change 2008-2012 (Mt C/yr⁻¹).

G Source: Table 4, SPM, SRLULUCF. Potential refers to the estimated net change in carbon stocks in 2010 (Mt C/yr⁻¹). The list of activities is not exclusive or complete, and it is unlikely that all countries will apply all activities. Some of these estimates reflect considerable uncertainty.

The CHAIRMAN. Thank you very much.
Dr. Hansen, welcome.

STATEMENT OF DR. JAMES E. HANSEN, DIRECTOR, GODDARD INSTITUTE FOR SPACE STUDIES, NATIONAL AERONAUTICS AND SPACE ADMINISTRATION

Dr. HANSEN. Thank you, Mr. Chairman.

I will talk about future climate. The most popular climate projection is the business-as-usual scenario. It leads to dramatic climate change later in the century. It provides a useful warning of what is possible if greenhouse gases grow more and more rapidly.

Four of my colleagues and I recently described an alternative scenario for climate change in the 21st Century which we think is a useful complement to the business-as-usual scenario. We assert that a brighter climate future is not only possible but can be achieved with actions that make good sense, independent of global warming.

This alternative scenario can be explained with the help of my bar chart for the forcing agents that underlie climate change. These are the climate forcings that exist today, relative to 1850. Carbon dioxide is the largest climate-forcing at 1.4 watts per meter squared, but these other greenhouse gases, methane, CFC's, low-level ozone, and nitrous oxide together cause a forcing that is equally as large. Methane, when you include its effects on other gases, causes a forcing half as large as CO_2, and then there are these aerosols. Aerosols are fine particles in the atmosphere, liquid or solid particles.

Black carbon, which comes from diesel fuel and coal-burning, causes a warming. Sulphate and organic carbon, which come from fossil fuel burning, cause cooling. All of these particles have some effect on cloud properties, which tends to cause a cooling. However, it is rather uncertain, the magnitude of that cooling.

The question is, how will these forcings change in the future? We could keep the additional climate forcing the next 50 years as small as 1 watt per meter squared by means of two actions. First, we must stop any further net growth of the non-CO_2 forcings, several of which are air pollution. Their growth needs to be stopped anyhow for reasons of public health. Second, CO_2 emissions can continue, but the emissions rate should be no larger than it is today, preferably declining slowly. The resulting forcing of 1 watt would be expected to cause some climate change, but less than 1 degree Celsius warming in 50 years.

So how can we stop the growth of these non-CO_2 forcings? Black carbon is a product of incomplete combustion. You can see it in the exhaust of diesel trucks. The microscopic particles are like tiny sponges. They soak up toxic organics and other aerosols. They are so tiny that when breathed in they penetrate human tissue deeply. Some of the smallest enter the bloodstream. These particulates cause respiratory and cardiac problems, asthma, acute bronchitis. With tens of thousands of deaths per year in the United States, also in Europe, where the health costs of particulate air pollution has been estimated at 1.6 percent of the gross domestic products.

In the developing world the costs are staggering. In India, approximately 270,000 children under the age of 5 die per year from acute respiratory infections caused by air pollution. Most of that pollution arises in household burning of field residue, cow dung, biomass, coal, for cooking and heating. There is now a brown cloud of pollution mushrooming from India. You can see it against the Himalayas.

There is a similar story for ozone. It is a pollutant that causes tens of billions of dollars of damage. We could stop its further growth. We have the technology to do that.

There is a somewhat different story for methane, but there are practical steps that could be taken to stop the growth of methane also.

The bottom line is that we have only one atmosphere, and it is a global atmosphere. My personal opinion is that we need to reduce the pollution that we are putting into it for a number of reasons, especially human health, and in the process we can help prevent the non-CO_2 climate forcing from increasing.

In the United States, for example, we could reduce diesel emissions and other soot emissions. We might also work with developing countries to help reduce their pollution. One possible long-term solution there would be electrification, a source of clean energy.

Finally, I must also address CO_2. It is the hardest part of the problem, but not as hard as it is often made out to be. In 1998, global CO_2 emissions declined slightly. In 1999 CO_2 emissions declined again. In 2000 I believe that they declined again, but the numbers are not yet in.

The CHAIRMAN. Doctor, why did those emissions decline?

Dr. HANSEN. The primary reason was China. Choking on its pollution, it reduced the amount of coal-burning, replaced coal power plants with gas power plants. Emissions from the United States actually increased in those years, but there are other countries where they are making efforts at renewable energies, and that is having some effect.

The CHAIRMAN. Thank you.

Dr. HANSEN. Now, that is just the trend that is needed to achieve our alternative scenario with only moderate climate change. In the near term, my opinion is that this trend can be maintained via concerted efforts toward increased energy efficiency and increased use of renewable energy sources. On the long-term, most energy experts suggest that we would need a significant increasing contribution from some energy source that produces little or no CO_2.

In my written testimony, I note several possibilities, which include zero emission coal, nuclear power, and a combination of solar energy and hydrogen and fuel cells. Each possibility has pros and cons, and I am not recommending policy. R&D is needed. It will be up to the public, via their representatives, to make choices. My point is that such possibilities exist, so the concept of the alternative scenario with only a modest climate change is a viable possibility.

Thank you. I would like to include in the record copies of my final three references in my official testimony. These discuss this topic in more detail, but in a plain language, which I think might be helpful.

[The prepared statement of Dr. Hansen follows:]

PREPARED STATEMENT OF DR. JAMES E. HANSEN, DIRECTOR, GODDARD INSTITUTE FOR SPACE STUDIES, NATIONAL AERONAUTICS AND SPACE ADMINISTRATION

1. PREFACE

Mr. Chairman and Members of the Committee: I appreciate the opportunity to clarify the paper I co-authored with four other scientists on climate change in the 21st century, published in *Proceedings of the National Academy of Sciences* (1). In that paper, we define an "alternative scenario" for the forcing agents that cause climate change. The alternative scenario gives equal emphasis to reducing air pollution and to a continued slow downtrend in CO_2 emissions. This scenario produces only a moderate climate change in the next 50 years. We suggest that the climate forcings in this scenario can be achieved via pragmatic actions that make good sense for a variety of reasons. Collateral benefits include improvements in human health, agricultural productivity, and greater energy self-sufficiency. Our alternative scenario differs markedly from the "business as usual" scenarios of the Intergovernmental Panel on Climate Change (IPCC), which have received the greatest attention among the plethora of IPCC scenarios. However, I emphasize that our paper is not a criticism of IPCC. The IPCC reports (2), produced by hundreds of outstanding scientists, provide an invaluable assessment of the status of scientific understanding of climate change.

Although our research has relevance to public issues, it is not our job to suggest policies. Our objective is to provide scientific information that the public and their representatives can use to help choose wise policies. Thus our aim is to provide relevant information on the forcing agents that drive climate change that is as quantitative and as clear as the data permit.

2. INTRODUCTION: BASIC CONCEPTS

The Earth's climate fluctuates from year to year and century to century, just as the weather fluctuates from day to day. It is a chaotic system, so changes occur without any forcing, but the chaotic changes are limited in magnitude. The climate also responds to forcings. If the sun brightens, a natural forcing, the Earth becomes warmer. If a large volcano spews aerosols into the stratosphere, these small particles reflect sunlight away and the Earth tends to cool. There are also human-made forcings.

We measure forcings in watts per square meter (W/m^2). For example, all the human-made greenhouse gases now cause a forcing of more than 2 W/m^2. It is as if we have placed two miniature Christmas tree bulbs over every square meter of the Earth's surface. That is equivalent to increasing the brightness of the sun by about 1 percent.

We understand reasonably well how sensitive the Earth's climate is to a forcing. Our most reliable measure comes from the history of the Earth. We can compare the current warm period, which has existed several thousand years, to the previous ice age, about 20,000 years ago (3, 4, 5). We know the composition of the atmosphere during the ice age from bubbles of air that were trapped as the ice sheets on Greenland and Antarctica built up from snowfall. There was less carbon dioxide (CO_2) and less methane (CH_4), but more dust in the air. The surface was different then, with ice sheets covering Canada and parts of Europe, different distributions of vegetation, even the coast-lines differed because sea level was 300 feet lower. These changes, as summarized in Figure 1, caused a negative climate forcing of about 6½ W/m^2. That forcing maintained a planet that was 5° C colder than today. This empirical information implies that climate sensitivity is about ¾° C per watt of forcing. Climate models have about the same sensitivity, which provides encouraging agreement between the real world and the complex computer models that we use to predict how climate may change in the future.

There is another important concept to understand. The climate cannot respond immediately to a forcing, because of the long time needed to warm the ocean. It takes a few decades to achieve just half of the equilibrium climate response to a forcing. Even in 100 years the response may be only 60–90 percent complete (5). This long response time complicates the problem for policy-makers. It means that we can put into the pipeline climate change that will only emerge during the lives of our children and grandchildren. Therefore we must be alert to detect and understand climate change early on, so that the most appropriate policies can be adopted.

3. PAST CLIMATE FORCINGS AND CLIMATE CHANGE

The climate forcings that exist today are summarized in Figure 2 (1). The greenhouse gases, on the left, have a positive forcing, which would tend to cause warming. CO_2 has the largest forcing, but CH_4, when its indirect effect on other gases is included, causes a forcing half as large as that of CO_2. CO_2 is likely to be increasingly dominant in the future, but the other forcings are not negligible.

Aerosols, in the middle of the figure, are fine particles in the air. Some of these, such as sulfate, which comes from the sulfur released in coal and oil burning, are white, so they scatter sunlight and cause a cooling. Black carbon (soot) is a product of incomplete combustion, especially of diesel fuel and coal. Soot absorbs sunlight and thus warms the planet. Aerosols tend to increase the number of cloud droplets, thus making the clouds brighter and longer-lived. All of the aerosol effects have large uncertainty bars, because our measurements are inadequate and our understanding of aerosol processes is limited.

If we accepted these estimates at face value, despite their large uncertainties, we would conclude that, climate forcing has increased by 1.7 W/m^2 since the Industrial Revolution began [the error bars, in some cases subjective, yield an uncertainty in the net forcing of 1 W/m^2]. The equilibrium warming from a forcing of 1.7 W/m^2 is 1.2–1.3° C. However, because of the ocean's long response time, we would expect a global warming to date of only about ¾° C. An energy imbalance of 0.7 W/m^2 remains with that much more energy coming into the planet than going out. This means there is another ½° C global warming already in the pipeline—it will occur even if atmospheric composition remains fixed at today's values.

The climate forcings are known more precisely for the past 50 years, especially during the past 25 years of satellite measurements. Our best estimates are shown in Figure 3. The history of the tropospheric aerosol forcing, which involves partial cancellation of positive and negative forcings, is uncertain because of the absence of measurements. However, the GHG and stratospheric aerosol forcings, which are large forcings during this period, are known accurately.

When we use these forcings in a global climate model (3) to calculate the climate change (6), the results are consistent with observations (Figure 4). We make five model runs, because of the chaos in the climate system. The red curve is the average of the five runs. The black dots are observations. The Earth's stratosphere cools as a result of ozone depletion and CO_2 increase, but it warms after volcanic eruptions. The troposphere and the surface warm because of the predominantly positive forcing by increases of greenhouse gases, in reasonably good agreement with observations.

The fourth panel in Figure 4 is important. It shows that the simulated planet has an increasing energy imbalance with space. There is more energy coming into the planet, from the sun, than there is energy going out. The calculated imbalance today is about 0.7 W/m^2. This, as mentioned above, implies that there is about 0.5° C additional global warming already in the pipeline, even if the atmospheric composition does not change further. An important confirmation of this energy imbalance has occurred recently with the discovery that the deep ocean is warming. That study (7) shows that the ocean took up heat at an average rate of 0.3 W/m^2 during the past 50 years, which is reasonably consistent with the predictions from climate models. Observed global sea ice cover has also decreased as the models predict.

There are many sources of uncertainty in the climate simulations and their interpretation. Principal among the uncertainties are climate sensitivity (the Goddard Institute for Space Studies model sensitivity is 3° C for doubled CO_2, but actual sensitivity could be as small as 2° C or as large as 4° C for doubled CO_2), the climate forcing scenario (aerosol changes are very poorly measured), and the simulated heat storage in the ocean (which depends upon the realism of the ocean circulation and mixing). It is possible to find other combinations of these "parameters" that yield satisfactory agreement with observed climate change. Nevertheless, the observed positive heat storage in the ocean is consistent with and provides some confirmation of the estimated climate forcing of 1.7 ± 1 W/m^2. Because these parameters in our model are obtained from first principles and are consistent with our understanding of the real world, we believe that it is meaningful to extend the simulations into the future, as we do in the following section. Such projections will become more reliable and precise in the future if we obtain better measurements and understanding of the climate forcings, more accurate and complete measures of climate change, especially heat storage in the ocean, and as we employ more realistic climate models, especially of ocean circulation.

4. SCENARIOS FOR 2000–2050

We extend our climate model simulations into the future for two climate forcing scenarios shown in Figure 5. In the popular "business-as-usual" scenario, which the media focuses upon, the climate forcing increases by almost 3 W/m^2 in the next 50 years. This leads to additional global warming of about 1.5° C by 2050 and several degrees by 2100. Such a scenario, with exponential growth of the greenhouse forcing, leads to predictions of dramatic climate change and serious impacts on society.

The "alternative scenario" assumes that global use of fossil fuels will continue at about today's rate, with an increase of 75 ppm in airborne CO_2 by 2050. Depending on the rate of CO_2 uptake by the ocean and biosphere this may require a small downtrend in CO_2 emissions, which would be a helpful trend for obtaining climate stabilization later in the century. The alternative scenario also assumes that there will be no net growth of the other forcings: in somewhat over-simplified terminology, "air pollution" is not allowed to get any worse that it is today. The added climate forcing in the alternative scenario is just over 1 W/m^2 in the next 50 years.

The alternative scenario results in an additional global warming in the next 50 years of about ¾° C, much less than for the business-as-usual scenario. In addition, the rate of stratospheric cooling declines in the alternative scenario (top panel of Figure 5), and in fact the lower stratospheric temperature would probably level out because of expected stratospheric ozone recovery (not included in this simulation). The planetary energy imbalance increases by only about ¼ W/m^2 in the alternative scenario, compared with almost 1 W/m^2 in the business-as-usual scenario. In other words, our children will leave their children a debt (¾° C additional warming in the pipeline) that is only slightly more than the amount of unrealized warming (½° C) hanging over our heads now.

Figure 6 is a cartoon summarizing the two parts of the alternative scenario. First, the scenario keeps the added CO_2 forcing at about 1 W/m^2, which requires that annual increases in atmospheric CO_2 concentrations be similar to those in the past decade. The precise scenario that we employ has the CO_2 growth rate declining slowly during these 50 years, thus making it more feasible to achieve still lower growth rates in the second half of the century and an eventual "soft landing" for climate change. Second, the net growth of other climate forcings is assumed to cease. The most important of these "other" forcings are methane, tropospheric ozone, and black carbon aerosols. Specific trace gas scenarios used in our global climate model simulations are shown in Figure 7.

In the following two sections we provide data that helps provide an indication of how difficult or easy it may be to achieve the elements of the alternative scenario.

5. ALTERNATIVE SCENARIO: AIR POLLUTION

One of the two requirements for achieving the alternative scenario is to stop the growth of non-CO_2 forcings. Principally, that means to halt, or even better reverse, the growth of black carbon (soot), tropospheric ozone (O_3) and methane (CH_4). These can loosely be described as air pollution, although in dilute amounts methane is not harmful to health. Black carbon, with adsorbed organic carbon, nitrates and sulfates, and tropospheric ozone are principal ingredients in air pollution.

Black carbon (soot). Black carbon aerosols, except in the extreme case of exhaust puffs from very dirty diesel trucks or buses, are invisibly small particles. They are like tiny sponges that soak up toxic organic material that is also a product of fossil fuel combustion. The aerosols are so small that they penetrate human tissue deeply when breathed into the lungs, and some of the tiniest particles enter the blood stream. Particulate air pollution, including black carbon aerosol, has been increasingly implicated in respiratory and cardiac problems. A recent study in Europe (8) estimated that air pollution caused annually 40,000 deaths, 25,000 new cases of chronic bronchitis, 290,000 episodes of bronchitis in children, and 500,000 asthma attacks in France, Switzerland and Austria alone, with a net cost from the human health impacts equal to 1.6 percent of their gross domestic product. Pollution levels and health effects in the United States are at a comparable level. Primary sources of black carbon in the West are diesel fuels and coal burning.

The human costs of particulate air pollution in the developing world are staggering. A study recently published (9) concluded that about 270,000 Indian children under the age of five die per year from acute respiratory infections arising from particulate air pollution. In this case the air pollution is caused mainly by low temperature inefficient burning of field residue, cow dung, biomass and coal within households for the purpose of cooking and heating. Pollution levels in China are comparably bad, but in China residential coal use is the largest source, followed by residential use of biofuels (10).

Referring back to Figure 2, note that there are several aerosols that cause cooling, in addition to black carbon that causes warming. There are ongoing efforts to slow the growth of sulfur emissions or reduce emissions absolutely, for the purpose of reducing acid rain. In our alternative scenario for climate forcings, it is assumed that any reduced sulfate cooling will be at least matched by reduced black carbon heating. Principal opportunities in the West are for cleaner more efficient diesel motors and cleaner more efficient coal burning at utilities. Opportunities in the developing world include use of biogas in place of solid fuels for household use, and eventually use of electrical energy produced at central power plants.

Ozone (O_3). Chemical emissions that lead to tropospheric ozone formation are volatile organic compounds and nitrogen oxides (carbon monoxide and methane also contribute). Primary sources of these chemicals are transportation vehicles, power plants and industrial processes.

High levels of ozone have adverse health and ecosystem effects. Annual costs of the impacts on human health and crop productivity are each estimated to be on the order of $10 billion per year in the United States alone.

Ozone in the free troposphere can have a lifetime of weeks, and thus tropospheric ozone is at least a hemispheric if not a global problem. Emissions in Asia are projected to have a small effect on air quality in the United States (11). Closer neighbors can have larger effects, for example, recent ozone increases in Japan are thought to be due in large part to combustion products from China, Korea and Japan (12). A coordinated reduction of those chemical emissions that lead to the formation of low level ozone would be beneficial to developing and developed countries.

Our alternative scenario assumes that it will be possible, at minimum, to stop further growth of tropospheric ozone. Recent evidence suggests that tropospheric ozone is decreasing downwind of regions such as Western Europe (13), where nitrogen oxide and carbon monoxide emissions are now controlled, but increasing downwind of East Asia (12). Global warming may aggravate summer time ozone production, but this feedback effect would be reduced with the small warming in the alternative scenario. The evidence suggests that cleaner energy sources and improved combustion technology could achieve an overall ozone reduction.

Methane (CH_4). Methane today causes a climate forcing half as large as that of CO_2, if its indirect effects on stratospheric H_2O and tropospheric O_3 are included. The atmospheric lifetime of CH_4 is moderate, only 8–10, years, so if its sources were reduced, the atmospheric amount would decline rather quickly. Therefore it offers a great opportunity for a greenhouse gas success story. It would be possible to stabilize atmospheric CH_4 by reducing the sources by about 10%, and larger reductions could bring an absolute decrease of atmospheric CH_4 amount.

The primary natural source of methane is microbial decay of organic matter under anoxic conditions in wetlands. Anthropogenic sources, which in sum may be twice as great as the natural source, include rice cultivation, domestic ruminants, bacterial decay in landfills and sewage, leakage during the mining of fossil fuels, leakage from natural gas pipelines, and biomass burning.

There are a number of actions that could be taken to reduce CH_4 emissions: (1) capture of methane in coal mining, landfills, and waste management, (2) reduction of pipeline leakage, especially from antiquated systems such as in the former Soviet Union, (3) reduction of methane from ruminants and rice growing, as the farmers' objectives are to produce meat, milk and power from the animals, not methane, and food and fiber from the fields, not methane.

The economic benefits of such methane reductions are not so great that they are likely to happen automatically. Methane reduction probably requires international cooperation, including developing countries. Although the task is nontrivial, it represents an opportunity for a success story. In some sense, methane in climate change is analogous to the role of methyl-chloroform in ozone depletion. Although the growth of long-lived chlorofluorocarbons has only begun to flatten out, stratospheric chlorine is already declining in amount because of reductions in the sources of short-lived methyl-chloroform.

6. ALTERNATIVE SCENARIO: CARBON DIOXIDE

CO_2 is the largest single human-made climate forcing agent today, and its proportion of the total human-made climate forcing can be anticipated to increase in the future. It is not practical to stop the growth of atmospheric CO_2 in the next several decades. However, it is possible to slow the growth rate of CO_2 emissions via actions that make good economic and strategic sense.

Scenarios for CO_2 are commonly constructed by making assumptions about population growth, standard of living increases, fuel choices, and technology. This procedure yields a huge range of possibilities with little guidance as to what is likely. An alternative approach is to examine historical and current rates of change of CO_2 emissions, estimate the changes that are needed to keep the climate change moderate, and consider actions that could produce such rates of change. That is the procedure we explore here.

Fossil-fuel CO_2 emissions. Figures 8 and 9 show U.S. and global CO_2 emissions. Emissions in the U.S. grew faster in the 1800s than in the rest of the world, as the U.S. itself was still growing and had rapid immigration. Growth of U.S. emissions was slower than in the rest of the world during the second half of the 20th century, when other parts of the world were industrializing.

The important period for the present discussion is the past 25 years, and the past decade. The U.S. growth rate was 1%/year over the past 25 years, as we largely succeeded in decoupling economic and energy use growth rates. The global growth rate was moderately higher, 1.4%, as there was faster growth in developing nations. However, in the past decade the growth rate of U.S. CO_2 emissions has been higher than in the world as a whole (1%/year in the U.S. vs. 0.6%/year in the world).

Figure 10 provides a useful summary. The U.S. portion of global fossil fuel CO_2 emissions increased from 10% in 1850 to 50% in 1920. Since then the U.S. portion has declined to 23% as other parts of the world industrialized. The temporary spike beginning in 1940 is associated with World War II, including vigorous exertion of U.S. industry to supply the war effort. In the 1990s the U.S. portion of global emissions increased, despite oratory about possible climate change and expectations that the developing world would be the source of increasing emissions.

Growth rate required for "alternative scenario". A small change in the CO_2 emissions growth rate yields large changes in emissions several decades in the future. A 1%/year growth yields a 64% growth of emissions in 50 years, compared with constant emissions (0%/year growth rate). A growth rate of −0.5%/year yields a −22% change of emissions in 50 years. Thus CO_2 emissions in 50 years are more than twice as large in a 1%/year scenario than in a −0.5%/year scenario.

Incomplete understanding of the Earth's "carbon cycle" creates some uncertainty, but to a good approximation the increase in atmospheric CO_2 is commensurate with the CO_2 emission rate. Therefore full achievement of the "alternative scenario" probably requires the global CO_2 emissions growth rate to be approximately zero or slightly negative over the next 50 years.

Even if the United States achieves a zero or slightly negative growth rate for CO_2 emissions, there is no guarantee that the rest of the world will follow suit. However, the economic and strategic advantages of a more energy efficient economy are sufficient to make this path attractive to most countries. It is likely that the shape of the U.S. and global CO_2 emissions curves will continue to be fundamentally congruent. In any case, any strategy for achieving a climate change "soft landing", whether pursued unilaterally or otherwise, surely requires that the downward change in the U.S. CO_2 emission growth rates be at least comparable to the change needed in the global average. There are many reasons for the United States to aggressively pursue the technology needed to achieve reduced CO_2 emissions, including potential economic benefit and reduced dependence on foreign energy sources.

It is not our task to suggest specific policies. However, we must make the case that there are options for achieving the slower CO_2 growth rate. Otherwise the alternative scenario is not viable.

In the short-term, a case can be made that pent-up slack in energy efficiency (14), if pursued aggressively, can help achieve a zero or slightly negative CO_2 emissions growth rate. Renewable energy sources, even though their output is relatively small, also can contribute to slowing the growth rate of emissions. There has been resistance of some industries to higher efficiency requirements. In that regard, the experience with chlorofluorocarbons is worth noting. Chemical manufacturers initially fought restrictions on CFC production, but once they changed their position and aggressively pursued alternatives they made more profits than ever. Similarly, if substantially improved efficiencies are developed (for air conditioners, appliances, etc.), such that there is a significant gap between operating costs of installed infrastructure and available technologies, that could facilitate increased turnover. Perhaps government or utility actions to encourage turnover also might be considered. Corporations will eventually reap large profits from clean air technologies, energy efficiency, and alternative energies, so it is important for our industry to establish a leadership position.

In the long-term, many energy analysts believe it is unlikely that energy efficiency and alternative energy sources can long sustain a global downtrend in CO_2 emissions. Lovins (15) argues otherwise, pointing out the cost competitiveness of efficient energy end-use, gas-fired cogeneration and trigeneration at diverse scales, wind power and other renewable sources. Certainly it makes sense to give priority to extracting the full potential from efficiency and renewable energy sources. Holdren (16) concludes that meeting the energy challenge requires that we maximize the capabilities and minimize the liabilities in the full array of energy options.

Many (my impression is, most) energy analysts believe that the requirement of a flat-to-downward trend of CO_2 emissions probably would require increasing penetration of a major energy source that produces little or no CO_2. Our task is only to argue that such possibilities exist. It will be up to the public, through their representatives, to weigh their benefits and liabilities. We mention three possibilities.

. *Nuclear power*: if its liabilities, including high cost and public concern about safety, waste disposal and nuclear weapons proliferation, can be overcome, it could provide a major no-CO_2 energy source. Advocates argue that a promising new generation of reactors is on the verge of overcoming these obstacles (17). There does not seem to be agreement on its potential cost competitiveness.

2. *Clean coal*: improved energy efficiency and better scrubbing of particulate emissions present an argument for replacing old coal-fired power plants with modern designs. However, CO_2 emissions are still high, so an increasing long-term role for coal depends on development of the "zero emissions" plant, which involves CO_2 capture and sequestration (18).

3. *Others*: Oppenheimer and Boyle (19) suggest that solar power, which contributes very little of our power at present, could become a significant contributor if it were used to generate hydrogen. The hydrogen can be used to generate electricity in a fuel cell. Of course the other energy sources can also be used to generate hydrogen.

In Holdren's (16) words: there are no silver bullets (in the array of energy options) nor are there any that we can be confident that we can do without. This suggests the need for balanced, increased public and private investment in research and development, including investments in generic technologies at the interface between energy supply and end use (20). The conclusion relevant to the alternative scenario is that, for the long-term, there are a number of possibilities for energy sources that produce no CO_2.

7. BENCHMARKS

The alternative scenario sets a target (1 W/m^2 added climate forcing in 50 years) that is much more ambitious than IPCC business-as-usual scenarios. Achievement of this scenario requires halting the growth of non-CO_2 climate forcings and slightly declining CO_2 emissions. Climate change is a long-term issue and strategies surely must be adjusted as evidence accumulates and our understanding improves. For that purpose it will be important to have quantitative measures of the climate forcings.

Non-CO_2 forcings. The reason commonly given for not including O_3 and soot aerosols in the discussions about possible actions to slow climate change is the difficulty in quantifying their amounts and sources. That is a weak argument. These atmospheric constituents need to be measured in all countries for the sake of human health. The principal benchmark for these constituents would be their actual amounts. At the same time, we must develop improved understanding of all the sources of these gases and aerosols, which will help in devising the most cost-effective schemes for reducing the climate forcings and the health impacts.

Methane, with an atmospheric lifetime of several years, presents a case that is intermediate between short-lived air pollutants and CO_2. Measurements of atmospheric amount provide a means of gauging overall progress toward halting its growth, but individual sources must be identified better to allow optimum strategies. Improved source identification is practical. In some cases quantification of sources can be improved by regional atmospheric measurements in conjunction with global tracer transport modeling.

Carbon Dioxide. Is it realistic to keep the CO_2 growth rate from exceeding that of today? The single most important benchmark will be the annual change of CO_2 emissions. The trend of CO_2 emissions by the United States is particularly important for the reasons discussed above. Figure 11 shows the United States record in the 1990s. The requirement to achieve the "alternative scenario" for climate forcings is that these annual changes average zero or slightly negative. It is apparent that, despite much rhetoric about global warming in the 1990s, CO_2 emissions grew at a rate that, if continued, would be inconsistent with the alternative scenario.

We suggest in the discussion above that it is realistic to aim for a lower emission rate that is consistent with the alternative scenario. This particular benchmark should receive much closer scrutiny than it has heretofore. The climate simulations and rationale presented above suggest that, if air pollution is controlled, the trend of this CO_2 benchmark, more than any other single quantity, can help make the difference between large climate change and moderate climate change.

8. COMMUNICATION

Our paper on the alternative scenario (1) was reported with a variety of interpretations in the media. As I discuss in an open letter (21), this may be unavoidable, as the media often have editorial positions and put their own spin on news stories.

Overall, the media correctly conveyed the thrust of our perspective on climate change. Furthermore, I suggest in my open letter that the *Washington Post* editorial on our paper (23) represented an astute assessment of the issues.

A basic problem is that we scientists have not informed the public well about the nature of research. There is no fixed "truth" delivered by some body of "experts". Doubt and uncertainty are the essential ingredient in science. They drive investigation and hypotheses, leading to predictions. Observations are the judge.

Of course, some things are known with higher confidence than others. Yet fundamental issues as well as details are continually questioned. The possibility of finding a new interpretation of data, which provides better insight into how something in nature works, is what makes science exciting. A new interpretation must satisfy all the data that the old theory fit, as well as make predictions that can be checked.

For example, the fact that the Earth has warmed in the past century is well established, and there is a high degree of confidence that humans have been a major contributor to this warming. However, there are substantial uncertainties about the contributions of different forcings and how these will change in the future.

In my open letter (21) I note the potential educational value of keeping an annual public scorecard of measured changes of (1) fossil fuel CO_2 emissions, (2) atmospheric CO_2 amount, (3) human-made climate forcing, and (4) global temperature. These are well-defined quantities with hypothesized relationships. It is possible to make the science understandable, and it may aid the discussions that will need to occur as years and decades pass. It may help us scientists too.

9. SUMMARY: A BRIGHTER FUTURE

The "business-as-usual" scenarios for future climate change provide a useful warning of possible global climate change, if human-made climate forcings increase more and more rapidly. I assert not only that a climatically brighter path is feasible, but that it is achievable via actions that make good sense for other reasons (22, 24). The alternative scenario that we have presented does not include a detailed strategic plan for dealing with global warming. However, it does represent the outline of a strategy, and we have argued that its elements are feasible.

It is impractical to stop CO_2 from increasing in the near term, as fossil fuels are the engine of the global economy. However, the decline of the growth rate of CO_2 emissions from 4 to 1%/year suggests that further reduction to constant emissions is feasible, especially since countries such as the United States have made only modest efforts at conservation. The potential economic and strategic gains from reduced energy imports themselves warrant the required efforts in energy conservation and development of alternative energy sources. It is worth noting that global CO_2 emissions declined in 1998 and again in 1999, and I anticipate that the 2000 data will show a further decline. Although this trend may not be durable, it is consistent with the alternative scenario.

The other requirement in our alternative scenario is to stop the growth of non-CO_2 forcings, which means, primarily, air pollution and methane. The required actions make practical sense, but they will not happen automatically and defining the optimum approach requires research.

A strategic advantage of halting the growth of non-CO_2 forcings is that it will make it practical to stop the growth of climate forcings entirely, in the event that climate change approaches unacceptable levels. The rationale for that claim is that an ever-growing fraction of energy use is in the form of clean electrical energy distributed by electrical grids. If improved energy efficiency and non-fossil energy sources prove inadequate to slow climate change, we may choose to capture CO_2 at power plants for sequestration.

Global warming is a long-term problem. Strategies will need to be adjusted as we go along. However, it is important to start now with common-sense economically sound steps that slow emissions of greenhouse gases, including CO_2, and air pollution. Early emphasis on air pollution has multiple immediate benefits, including the potential to unite interests of developed and developing countries. Barriers to energy efficiency need to be removed. Research and development of alternative energies should be supported, including a hard look at next generation nuclear power. Ultimately strategic decisions rest with the public and their representatives, but for that reason we need to make the science and alternative scenarios clearer.

REFERENCES

. Hansen, J., M. Sato, R. Ruedy, A. Lacis and V. Oinas, Global warming in the twenty-first century: an alternative scenario, *Proc. Natl. Acad. Sci.*, 97, 9875–9880, 2000.

2. Intergovernmental Panel on Climate Change, *Climate Change 1995*, J.T. Houghton, L.G. Meira Filho, B.A. Callandar, N Harris, A. Kattenberg and K. Maskell (eds.), Cambridge Univ. Press, Cambridge, England, 572 pp., 1996; Intergovernmental Panel on Climate Change, *Climate Change 2000*, editors . . . 2001.

3. Hansen, J., R. Ruedy, A. Lacis, M. Sato, L. Nazarenko, N. Tausnev, I. Tegen and D. Koch, in *General Circulation Model Development*, ed. D. Randall, Academic Press, New York, pp. 127–164, 2000.

4. Hoffert M.I. and C.Covey, Deriving global climate sensitivity from paleoclimate reconstructions, *Nature*, 360, 573–576, 1992.

5. Hansen, J., A. Lacis, D. Rind, G. Russell, P. Stone, I. Fung, R. Ruedy and J. Lerner, Climate sensitivity: analysis of feedback mechanisms, *Geophys. Mono.*, 29, 130–163, 1984.

6. Hansen, J. et al., Climate forcings in the GISS SI2000 model, to be submitted to *J. Geophys. Res.*, 2001.

7. Levitus, S., J.I. Antonov, T.P. Boyer and C. Stephens, Warming of the world ocean, *Science*, 287, 2225–2229, 2000.

8. Kunzil, N., R. Kaiser, S. Medina, M. Studnicka, O. Chanel, P. Filliger, M. Herry, F. Horak, V. Puybonnieux-Texier, P. Quenel, J. Schneider, R. Seethaler, J.C. Vergnaud and H. Sommer, Public health impact of outdoor and traffic-related air pollution: a European assessment, *The Lancet*, 356, 795–801, 2000.

9. Smith, K.R., National burden of disease in India from indoor air pollution, *Proc. Natl. Acad. Sci.*, 97, 13286–13293, 2000.

0. Streets, D.G., S. Gupta, S.T. Waldhoff, M.Q. Wang, T.C. Bond and B. Yiyun, Black carbon emissions in China, *Atmos. Envir.*, in press, 2001.

1. Jacob, D.J., J.A. Logan and P.P. Murti, Effect of rising Asian emissions on surface ozone in the United States, *Geophys. Res. Lett.*, 26, 2175–2178, 1999.

2. Lee, S.H., H. Akimoto, H. Nakane, S. Kurnosenko and Y. Kinjo, Lower tropospheric ozone trend observed in 1989–1998 at Okinawa, Japan, *Geophys. Res. Lett.*, 25, 1637–1640, 1998.

3. Simmonds, P.G., S. Seuring, G. Nickless and R.G. Derwent, Segregation and interpretation of ozone and carbon monoxide measurements by air mass origin at the TOR station Mace Head, Ireland from 1987 to1995, *J. Atmos. Chem.*, 28, 45–59, 1997.

4. Brown, M.A., The role of CO_2 gases in climate policy, workshop of United States Association for Energy Economics, Washington, DC, October 16, 2000.

5. Lovins, A.B. and L. Hunter Lovins, *Climate: Making Sense and Making Money*, Rocky Mountain Institute, Snowmass, CO, http://www.rmi.org/images/other/C-/ClimateMSMM.pdf; Hawken, P.G., A.B. Lovins and L.H. Lovins, *Natural Capitalism*, Little Brown, NY, 1997, www.natcap.org.

6. Holdren, J.P., Meeting the energy challenge, *Science*, 291, 945, 2001.

7. Wald, M.L., Industry gives nuclear power a second look, *New York Times*, April 24, 2001.

8. Ecoal, Harnessing energy with reduced emissions to atmosphere—the pace of research to generate dynamic solutions for coal, *World Coal Institute Newsletter*, 36, December, 2000; also see Williams, R.H., presentation at symposium at Nuclear Control Institute, Washington, DC, April 9, 2001..

9. Oppenheimer, M. and R.H. Boyle, Dead Heat, Basic Books, New York, 1990.

20. Nakicenovic, N., A. Grübler and A. McDonald, *Global Energy Perspectives*, Cambridge Univ. Press, Cambridge, U.K. 1998.

21. Hansen, J., An open letter on global warming, http://naturalscience.com/ns/letters/ns—let25.html.

22. Hansen, J., A brighter future, *Clim. Change*, in press, 2001.

23. Anonymous, Hot news on global warming, *Washington Post*, page A18, August 28, 2000.

24. Hansen, J., Try a common-sense response to global warming, *International Herald Tribune*, Nov. 16, 2000.

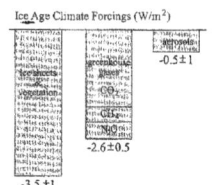

Figure 1. Climate forcing during the Ice Age 20,000 years ago relative to the current interglacial period. This forcing of -6.6 ±1.5 W/m² and the 5°C cooling of the Ice Age imply a climate sensitivity of 0.75°C per 1 W/m².

$Forcing \sim 6.6 \pm 1.5 \ W/m^2$
$Observed \ \Delta T \sim 5 \ °C$
$\rightarrow \frac{3}{4} \ °C \ per \ W/m^2$

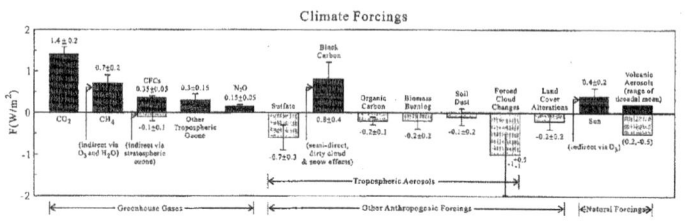

Figure 2. Estimated change of climate forcings between 1850 and 2000, based on (1) with five principal aerosols delineated.

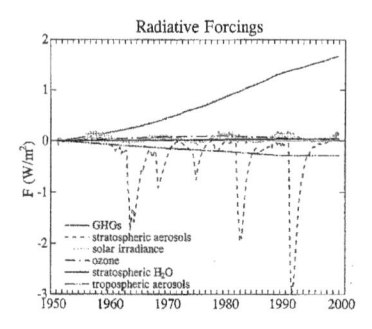

$Sum \sim 1.7 \ W/m^2$
$Sensitivity \ \frac{3}{4} \ °C \ per \ W/m^2 \rightarrow 1.2 - 1.3 \ °C \ warming \ at \ equilibrium$
$Today: \frac{3}{4} \ °C \ warming + 0.7 \ W/m^2 \ remaining \ imbalance$

Figure 3. Climate forcings in the past 50 years, relative to 1950, due to six mechanisms (6). The first five forcings are based mainly on observations, with stratospheric H₂O including only the source due to CH₄ oxidation. GHGs include the well-mixed greenhouse gases, but not O₃ and H₂O. The tropospheric aerosol forcing is uncertain in both its magnitude and time dependence.

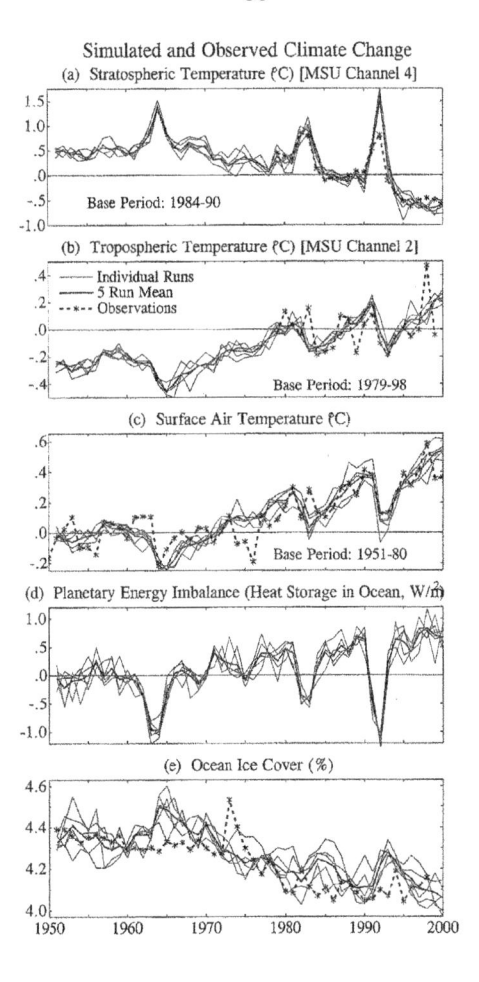

Figure 4. Simulated and observed climate change for 1950-2000 (6). These simulations with GISS climate model (3) employ empirical mixing rates and fixed horizontal heat transports in the ocean (5). Climate forcings are those of Figure 3.

(a) Stratospheric Temperature (°C) [MSU Channel 4]

* Observations

(b) Surface Air Temperature (°C)

Business-As-Usual
Alternative Scenario

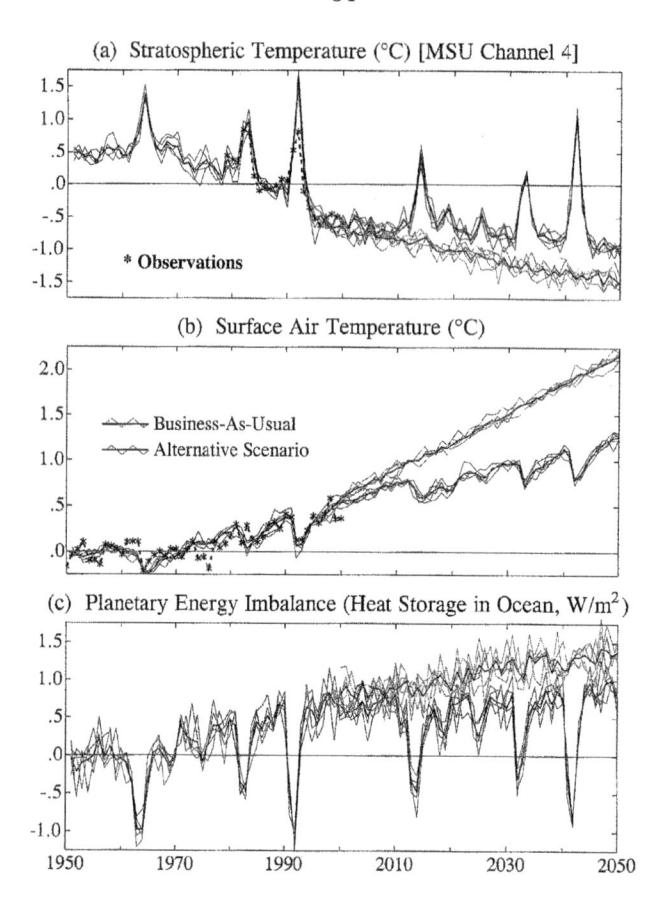

(c) Planetary Energy Imbalance (Heat Storage in Ocean, W/m^2)

Figure 5. Simulated temperatures and planetary energy imbalance for the forcings in Figure 3 (6). The business-as-usual (1% CO_2/year) adds 2.9 W/m^2 forcing in 2001-2050. The alternative scenario adds a greenhouse gas forcing of 1.1 W/m^2 in that period and includes volcanoes similar to those during 1951-2000.

Figure 6. Cartoon depicting approximate added climate forcings between in an extreme "business-as-usual" scenario and the "alternative" scenario.

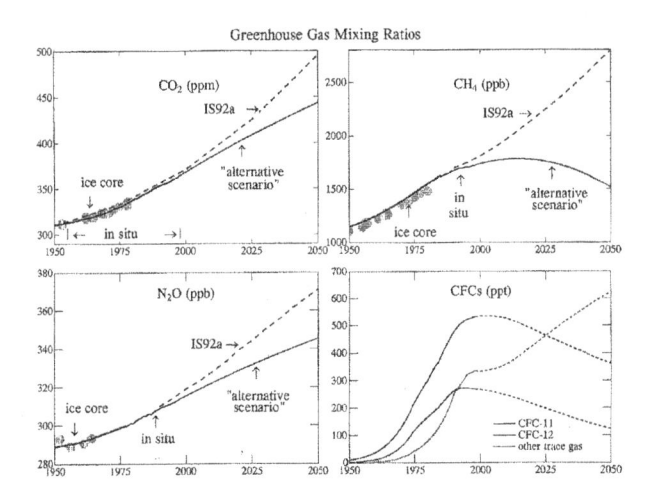

Figure 7. Measured greenhouse gas amounts and "alternative scenario" extensions to 2050. IS92a scenarios of IPCC (2) for CO_2, CH_4 and N_2O are illustrated for comparison. The sum of CFC and "other trace gas" forcings is constant after 2000 in the alternative scenario.

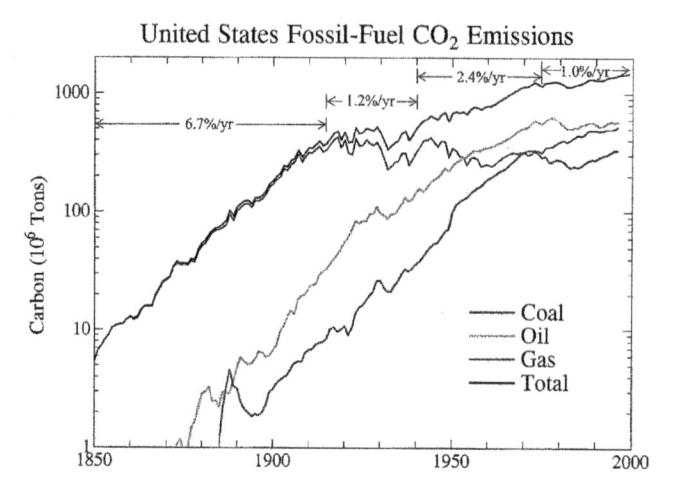

Figure 8. Annual emissions of CO_2 from fossil fuels in the United States (principal data source: Oak Ridge National Laboratory, Department of Energy)

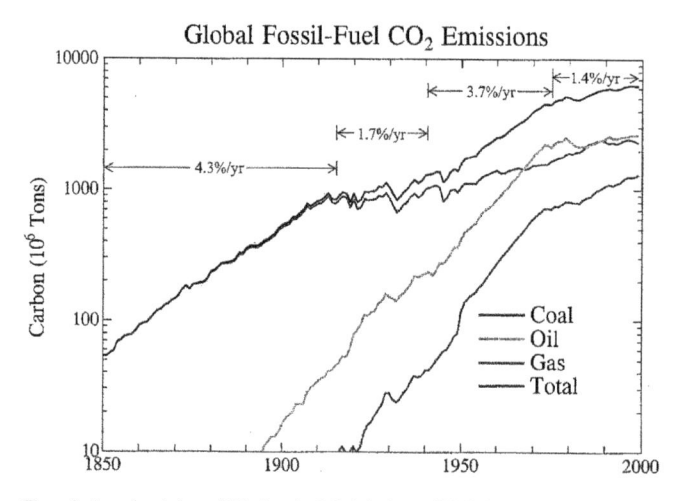

Figure 9. Annual emissions of CO_2 from fossil fuels in the world (principal data source: Oak Ridge National Laboratory, Department of Energy)

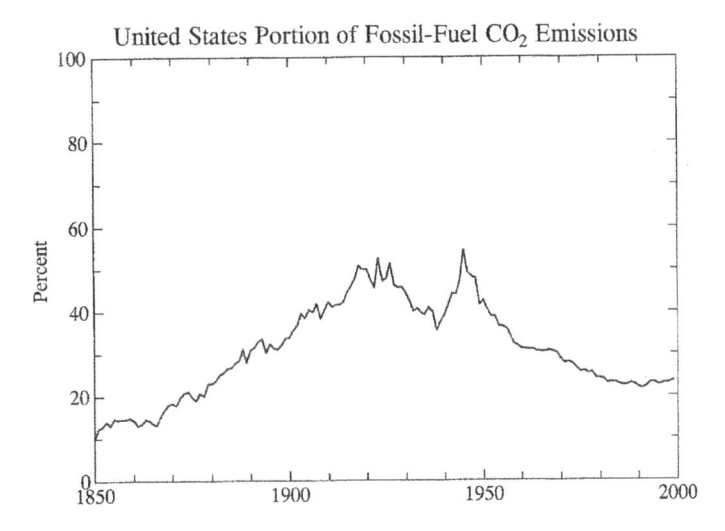

Figure 10. Percentage of world fossil-fuel CO_2 emissions produced in the United States.

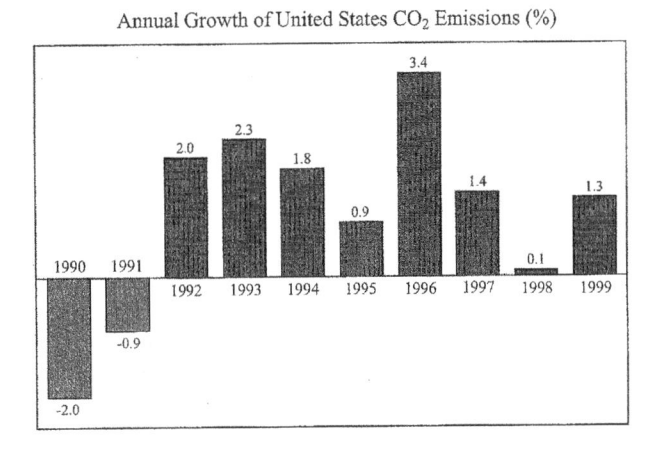

Figure 11. Annual change of United States fossil-fuel CO_2 emissions.

The CHAIRMAN. Thank you, Dr. Hansen. I want to thank all the witnesses for being here. Dr. Lindzen, you said we need to support science without promoting alarmism. How do you do that, and if you would speak close to the mike.

Dr. LINDZEN. A good question. It seems to me that to some extent that will require more trust of the scientific community. Essentially, in the post war period you typically had from the Armed Forces 5-year grants covering significant numbers of scientists, minimal paperwork, and so on.

This was a very productive period for science. As you ask for more direct evidence of relevance, the easiest form of relevance becomes alarm, and you encourage a kind of bad trend. I do not have an easy answer to it, but I think it is something that should be thought out. You do not want bias built into your scientific support system.

The CHAIRMAN. Thank you. It is my understanding that all five members of the panel have been involved in the IPCC report. Dr. Lindzen said that hundreds of scientists were never asked, that the report was changed in Shanghai, and that significant pressure was exerted. I would like to hear the other four witnesses' response to those rather serious statements.

Dr. Ramaswamy, we will begin with you, sir.

Dr. RAMASWAMY. I think—and this is going to be a long-winded answer, but the transfer of what is in the detailed technical chapter report, the transfer of that information to the summary for policymakers admittedly involves lots of careful choices of words and sentences and phrases, because it has to be a short summary, and so doubtless, you know, some of the information that is in the chapters will not appear in the summary.

But I must say I was there in Shanghai. I was there in the plenary, and I believe there were lead authors from—I have not checked carefully, but I think the lead authors from all the chapters were present at the meeting in Shanghai. The way the deliberations went concerning the summary for policymakers: First of all, the draft was drawn up by scientists; any changes that were to be introduced in Shanghai—if changes were to be introduced, it was only in response to some comments.

If some reviewer had comments, or someone on the floor had some comments, then there were considerations of how the words had been crafted, how the sentence had been crafted, and after that the scientists had to agree, basically, on any language that went in.

If the scientists objected, that language never made its appearance, and so I believe that scientists did contribute significantly to the sense expressed in the summary for policymakers. Admittedly not all the scientists were involved in the drafting process of the chapters there, but by and large there was a representation from, I believe, all the chapters there, so this was pretty important, because these scientists——

The CHAIRMAN. Was there pressure exerted to change the report?

Dr. RAMASWAMY. No, there was no pressure exerted as far as I know. I was there on the floor on all the days, and there was no pressure exerted. In fact, there were moments when language that somebody would insist on was totally vetoed by the scientists, and that was the final word. Because the scientists did not like it that wording did not go in. Having said that, I would think it is true to say that not everything that is in the chapters did come through in the summary for policymakers, but these were by and large what I would call details with respect to certainties or uncertainties, not the major points.

So for example, Dr. Lindzen mentioned the uncertainty we have about water vapor and clouds and climate feedbacks, and that is a very prominent uncertainty, and that was recognized in the summary for policymakers.

So as I said at the outset, there is a problem in trying to use the English language to condense 1,000 pages down to 15 or 20 pages, but I do not believe that the principal findings were in any way muted in the transfer from the chapters to the summary.

The CHAIRMAN. Dr. Sathaye.

Dr. SATHAYE. Yes, thank you, Mr. Chairman. I think it might be worth explaining very briefly the process we go through in order to arrive at the Summary for Policymakers. Each of the chapters has an Executive Summary that is prepared with full participation of all the authors who have worked on that chapter. That Executive Summary is then used to produce two documents. One is the Technical Summary and the other is the Summary for Policymakers, and they have different audiences.

You do not necessarily want all of the technical material we put in the Technical Summary to appear in the Summary for Policymakers, which is intended for a completely different audience. We often have a lot more material in the Technical Summary which need not appear in the Summary for Policymakers, and this certainly was the case with the Working Group III report.

The CHAIRMAN. I understand that, doctor, but my question was, were hundreds of scientists never asked and was it changed in Shanghai? Was there pressure brought to bear on those who were drafting the report?

Dr. SATHAYE. I worked on the Working Group III Report, which did not meet in Shanghai, but the process was very similar, and at no point in time was there pressure brought on any of the authors to change any of their findings. Indeed, as Ram just mentioned, in Akra, delegates consulted us. They made sure that the language we were using was accurate, and we made changes to that language to make sure that it fully reflected the underlying report.

The CHAIRMAN. Thank you.

Dr. McCarthy.

Dr. MCCARTHY. Thank you. I would just echo the comments of my two colleagues. I was in Shanghai, the working group that I chair had its final plenary meeting in Geneva. The process that was just described was the same for Working Group 2. The actual drafting of the Summary for Policymakers (SPM) was done by about 60 authors, but every author had an opportunity to see each draft as it was initially prepared before a meeting of all authors last August. Everyone had a chance to look at the responses to the government reviews and every author had an opportunity to see the revisions to the SPM.

We took the revised form of the SPM to our plenary meeting in Geneva, and I would describe the process as one of trying to take, as mentioned by my colleagues, a document that is full of the representation of scientific detail first to a summary document, the Technical Summary, and then to as clear a statement as scientists can produce—that is, strip all the jargon, to make the language of the Summary for Policymakers intelligible to anyone who would care to know how this information might be used in a policy context. So I see the plenary, really, as the final clarifying process.

Now, similarly, we had about 40 of our authors—that is, our lead authors of every chapter present at that final meeting. If at any time a question was made, or raised from the floor of the plenary, by any of the 150 delegates from 100 nations, about a particular statement, saying for example, that they thought it should be worded differently, if the suggested change was simply for the purpose of clarifying the language, and the authors present concurred that the proposed change did not alter the scientific meaning, then the suggestion would stand.

At times a suggestion by a delegate from one country would be opposed by another saying no, I do not think that makes it clearer at all, so a lot of our discussion went back and forth involving maybe a third delegate, who came up with yet another suggestion, and if we got stuck in a situation like this, then the chair would ask a small group to retire during lunch and have a smaller meeting, open to everyone, but asking someone to chair it, and then to come back to the full plenary with a proposed solution.

So literally, the process is one in which we never vote. We would proceed through the document until at the end of the day all delegations say, I am satisfied I fully understand this document, it is gaveled, and it is then fully accepted by the plenary.

The CHAIRMAN. Dr. Hansen.

Dr. HANSEN. That is a very difficult question. The IPCC is carrying out a very necessary process, and the technical work is superb. It involves a large number of outstanding scientists, and I am in no way critical of those scientists, but I must say I have a significant degree of discomfort with the extrapolation of the science into policy directions, the close interconnection of the IPCC and the Kyoto discussions.

I also think that a large committee is seldom the best approach for determining actions. I do not feel that I have a prescription or that I know the best procedure to do this, but I felt much more comfortable with the assessment 20 years ago when it was done by the National Academy of Sciences, a stellar committee chaired by Joel Charney of MIT, who stayed away from policy but gave an outstanding scientific assessment.

So I do not have a very good answer to that, but I feel some discomfort about it.

The CHAIRMAN. Thank you. I would like to ask one more question of the panel, and this is something which I am sure will not be an easy one or a comfortable one for you to respond to. I want you to for a moment put yourself in the shoes of the legislator. We have now received numerous reports. We now have cumulative evidence that there is climate change. We have had some disagreements on what should be done, if anything, and so I would like to begin with you, Dr. Lindzen, and ask you, as a legislator, what policies or what legislation would you propose to attempt to address these issues, if any? Perhaps none.

Dr. LINDZEN. I think it may be premature to take actions explicitly designed for this. I think there is general agreement with taking care of things like efficiency, reduced toxic pollution and so on, which have independent benefits. This is, I think, what is referred to as no regrets. I think with respect to science, treat it as an open question and ask that the physics be improved.

At present, I mean, it is a point I make in my testimony, it is widely understood that doubling CO_2 alone gives you about a degree centigrade warming. The rest of the higher predictions come from the so-called feedback processes. These are very weakly understood. They are crucial, and they are in many ways not the focus of our research. I think they deserve more.

The CHAIRMAN. Dr. Ram.

Dr. RAMASWAMY. Well, that is a difficult question, and I guess I am going to stick to my parochial barriers here and essentially emphasize—in fact, I would reiterate Dr. Lindzen's point, that good, sound science should be the underpinning for any policy decision, and the science should be checked and rechecked constantly, because science is an evolving thing. It is advancing all the time.

So there should be a careful scrutiny of the science, and I would emphasize that besides the measurements we also need process studies and modeling to go along with it. The three actually go simultaneously together.

You cannot have a decision based on just observations. You cannot have a decision just based on models alone, and I think it is this collective picture, looking at all the observations and indicators, coupled with model simulations, and coupled with the understanding of the physical processes, that essentially unites and completes the picture. If you had just one of them, that is not the whole picture, so I would emphasize that that be the underpinning for the policy decisions.

I know this is not the direct answer to your question, but it is kind of in a roundabout way.

The CHAIRMAN. Dr. Sathaye.

Dr. SATHAYE. Well, never having been a legislator, this is a tough question to answer, but since the work that I do focuses a lot on technologies and costs and policies, let me just suggest a few areas which are, as others have mentioned before me, worth pursuing regardless. It is very clear that energy efficiency improvements and long-term R&D would form the backbone of any decisions you might make, if not today, perhaps some years from now, and in fact the question about how soon do you wish to act, or one should act, depends a lot upon what levels you wish to stabilize climate at, for which we do not have a consensus.

If you want to stabilize at 450, you need to start reducing emissions by 2015, and so forth, and so without having that particular consensus, one pursues other things that are good for the economy, and I do not think we are doing nearly enough in that area.

The CHAIRMAN. Do you not think that there is largely an emerging consensus on this issue?

Dr. SATHAYE. Yes, there is an emerging consensus on this issue. The sooner there is consensus, or the lower your emissions are, the sooner you will act; the more room you will have to play later on, so to speak.

The CHAIRMAN. Dr. McCarthy.

Dr. MCCARTHY. Thank you, Mr. Chairman.

The CHAIRMAN. By the way, I am aware this is a very difficult question and I ask it of myself every day.

Dr. MCCARTHY. Some of us took the easy route and retired to an academic life, rather than the difficult route, that of a legislator.

I think that there are several things we can and should do right away. I think some of these suggestions have been made already by my colleagues taking the lead from Dr. Hansen on no-regrets policies.

I think the notion that there may be some low-hanging fruit with some of the other greenhouse gases should be explored vigorously, but I do believe that this is an issue that we should look at very differently today than just 5 or even 10 years ago, because as the Summary for Policymakers in this third assessment says for the impacts of climate change, we know now about impacts, things we did not know 5 years ago because of the recent rate of some of these changes.

With respect to the comments made by Senator Stevens, I would comment that one of my hobbies is the old polar exploration literature. It would be fair to say if someone had told me 5 years ago that we would be seeing within the next 10, 20, 30 years the opportunity for ships to travel through the Northwest Passage, I would have said that is inconceivable. Historically, this name has been a misnomer. It should have been called the Northwest impediment.

The fact that we have seen these dramatic changes, and they are entirely consistent, as I have said, where we have examined thousands of papers, and for 80 percent of them, these changes are consistent with the local changes in temperature. This tells us that responses to climate change are occurring more quickly than we had thought possible.

Now, I know Dr. Lindzen said we do not understand the physics, and I certainly do not understand the physics, but Working Group 1 tells us that intense heat spells, intense precipitation events, increased wind velocities associated with tropical storms, and increased El Niño like conditions are all projections for future climate with 90 percent confidence.

Now, I am not an expert on that. I cannot possibly explain the mechanism, but that is part of the summary statement from the Working Group 1 report. If we are wrong and find that these factors are not so serious, then we could feel comfort in having sat aside and waiting for clearer signals. But if we are wrong in the other direction and if they are even more serious than we think they are, then these consequences could be even larger.

I think an appropriate way to look at this is rather like insurance, the insurance that we invest in for all of our personal property, and our lives. I think that to gamble that these projections will not be borne out within the near future is a very, very risky step, and I believe, as our report says very clearly, that even the most aggressive actions that have been proposed will not prevent some of this damage. In addition to looking very seriously at all mitigation options, we must look very seriously at enhancing opportunities for adaptation, not only in those regions that are going to be most hard-hit, the tropic and subtropical regions, but also in northern industrialized countries as well.

The CHAIRMAN. Dr. Hansen.

Dr. HANSEN. I agree that first of all we should take the steps that have other benefits and, in fact, I think these may take us most of the way and perhaps all of the way to what we need. I refer particularly to pollution, the examples I gave with regard to air pollution. Also, we need to support energy efficiency and alternative energies, because of the strategic value they will have with regard to our energy independence. Second, we should make the measurements that are necessary so we can understand what is really happening to the climate system. Third, we need to adapt the approach as we go along. This is a long-term issue.

The CHAIRMAN. Thank you. There is a vote on. Senator Brownback is over voting, and he will be back for his questions. I am going to go vote and will be back. Senator Kerry, do you want to start?

Senator KERRY. Is Senator Brownback going to come back?

The CHAIRMAN. Yes, or I can recess.

Senator KERRY. Why don't we recess, and I will come back, too.

The CHAIRMAN. We will take a brief recess. Senator Kerry and Senator Brownback will come back. Senator Kerry will have questions as soon as he returns. He is very quick.

[Recess.]

Senator BROWNBACK. If we could bring the committee back to order, sorry about the brief intermission. We have a vote on on the floor, and we will continue with the hearing, if you do not mind. Let me make a couple of comments, if I could to you, and ask that my full opening statement be put into the record, at the appropriate place in the record. I appreciate the testimony you gentlemen have given and the information you have put forward.

I have put forward two bills that I think are in lines with the keeping of some of the items that you have suggested, and I just want to draw your attention to it and then ask your comments about it. Number 1 is a domestic carbon bill that would make small payments to farmers, primarily, on the basis of practices that they would use that would increase CO_2 or carbon sequestration in the soil.

These I think would be generally practices along the lines of a no-regrets policy, as one of you had identified that would approve soil conservation, soil quality by putting back into the soil carbon, which has been released when we tilled up the prairies, when we have gone to plowing previously, and this would be coming back to more of a no-till, more fixing the carbon into the soil, so that you would reward farmers for a process of farming, not necessarily production of farming, but a process by which they would farm that would fix more carbon in the soil, and these would be the practices that would be agreed to by appropriate scientific and USDA models and panels.

The second item is a bill that provides for $200 million in tax credits to individuals or companies in the United States that invest in reforestation, either domestic or abroad. This is modeled after what I think is a start of a pretty successful-looking project by the Nature Conservancy in South America. They have got projects going in Belize, Bolivia, and Brazil. I am hoping they will get outside of just B countries and into all nations.

I toured one in January in Brazil, where they had bought back about 150,000 acres in the Atlantic forest region in Brazil that had been broken out, farmed, and then had returned to pasture for water buffalo, and they were buying it back to turn it back to Atlantic forest region. They were measuring the amount of carbon that was being fixed over a 40-year cycle, working with the local nongovernmental organization in Brazil that actually owned the land. The money was put up by groups in the United States, several large companies that put the resources up to actually purchase the property.

What I would do is provide tax credits, about $200 million initially, to try to incentivize and encourage more of these reforestation carbon-fixing, or carbon sinks, as I have addressed it in both types of models.

I would be curious what you think about these sort of incentivized—and I would like to think along the lines in the future, sa we reduce CO_2, that we will do so on a market basis, where we do it on a least-cost type of models, that these would be kind of early types of models where you get the low-lying fruit of pretty quick CO_2 sinks, sequestrations that would take place with these.

Any thoughts about models like this from any of the panelists, or if you yourself have thought along any of these policy models?

Dr. Sathaye.

Dr. SATHAYE. Yes, I think—let me speak with a personal—from a scientific perspective on this topic. We had an IPCC report on forestry that looked at many of the questions related to project-specific soil conservation. I think at the outset I should say yes, it is a great idea, and that it is worth pursuing.

Certainly land exchange and forestry options offer an important sink for carbon, and the no-till agriculture you mentioned would be one of the types of activities that could be done in the United States and in other countries as well. Indeed, in many cases these types of projects have the potential to bring in early monetary returns for the investor.

As the trees grow, and if you are in a position to sell that carbon, you can get revenues fairly early on, and it is a good thing for these types of projects.

There are two issues, though, that one needs to be careful about in pursuing these projects. One has to do with a question of permanence, and this, too, has been alluded to by many. One of the challenges is, how long would these carbon sinks last? We lose carbon at some point in time. We have four different ways of dealing with that, and to the extent that these projects incorporate one of those four ways, then you can, indeed, pursue these kinds of projects.

The four ways are, they all amount really to accounting for any carbon that you lose and this may be done through an insurance scheme, it may be done by simply starting another project in place of whatever carbon you might lose, so there are different approaches to it. Well, we know how to deal with it.

The second issue has to deal with what is being labeled as leakage, and this is where, if you practice, let us say, reducing deforestation in a given area, and if they go to some other place and start deforesting, then you lose any carbon benefits you might get in the area that you stopped the deforestation from. How do you avoid that?

Here, too, we have ways to address leakage by pursuing multicomponent projects. You have wide deforestation in one area, then you can provide incentives in another area, so we have ways of dealing with this, and to the extent we take care of those, these are as good an approach for removing carbon out of the atmosphere as we might get out of energy efficiency, or alternative energy sources.

Senator BROWNBACK. Others? Dr. Hansen, did you have any thoughts on this, perchance?

Dr. HANSEN. Well, on the face of it they are both commendable activities. It does depend upon the kind of detail we were just hearing about, and I think it is important to quantify the degree to which these other benefits in addition to reducing CO_2 in the air, are in fact realized. We need to have a good cost-benefit analysis. Even though I am from Iowa, I do not claim to have expertise on exactly what the impact will be, of either the no-till or the reforestation, because of these possible indirect effects. So I cannot really say much now that can help you.

Senator BROWNBACK. Dr. McCarthy.

Dr. MCCARTHY. Just briefly, Senator Brownback, I, too, believe that this is an example of the sort of incentive the government can provide that could in some instances make a substantial difference.

It has, however, only been within the last, maybe handful of years that scientists have begun to look rather rigorously at some of these balances and the effects of perturbations, and the cessation of a perturbation on an ecosystem, but it is very clear that that is an area that has potential to be an important contributor, and I would just add that it is also important to keep in mind—I am not directing this to you personally, but to all of us, that there is no single best way to address the sort of larger question we are asking, and I think this is an example of mitigation options that people would not have thought of a decade ago as having any potential.

Within the last 5 years we have begun to look at it carefully. It appears now that with the sort of qualifications my colleagues have mentioned, that it does have potential and should be looked at very carefully.

Senator BROWNBACK. Dr. Sathaye, is this the sort of thing that could possibly be used in emissions trading? You talk somewhat about emissions trading, and least-cost approaches for CO_2 reductions. Would you, particularly on reforestation efforts, support the use of that on an emissions trading type of basis?

Dr. SATHAYE. First of all, yes, you could include reforestation options in the emissions trading scheme but the way it is being discussed, and the way it has been talked about, is to have reforestation projects in other countries, and then trade—let us say you do a reforestation project in Europe some place, or Asia, the carbon that you sequester through that process could be traded with carbon needs here.

That is certainly a legitimate way of doing it, and it could be identical, to what you would get from any other type of energy source.

A couple of caveats that I mentioned earlier about permanence, and also this question of how carefully can you measure carbon. We have carbon in four different pools. In the forestry projects, we have it in vegetation, in soils, in products, and in above and below-ground vegetation, litter and so forth. These are the pools.

Senator BROWNBACK. Those are being measured in the Bolivia and the Brazilian project pretty aggressively, and I do not know if the scientific community has agreed to the measurement method that they want to go with, but they are measured on a first year, third year, and then every fifth year, then on through 40 years to try to address a permanence issue, and leakage issue is also addressed in the bill, requiring to work with local people to encourage them to be able to stay, but shift their economic income sources from what they have been in the past.

Dr. SATHAYE. There is no difficulty in measurement methods. We know how to measure carbon. If somebody brought it to my lab and said, "measure this carbon, from this soil," or "we can do it." The challenge is really whether we have a system set up in order to do these kinds of measurements on a normal basis, and how much might this cost.

Senator BROWNBACK. The final question I want to ask, Dr. Hansen, you mentioned something about a clean coal type of technology, and I think this is also in another testimony, where you actually capture the CO_2 at the end of the pipe, I guess, and store it, is that correct?

Dr. HANSEN. Yes. The danger with coal is that it is by far the largest potential source of atmospheric CO_2, with about 10 times as much as oil and gas. So you have to be very careful about introducing greater coal use. We can reduce the black carbon probably fairly easily, that is the soot, with more efficient burning and filters on the smokestacks. In fact, that would do some good, but if we then start burning so much coal that we are producing more and more CO_2, that would be counterproductive. So it is, I think, important to explore this possibility of zero emissions coal, but again I am not an expert on that.

I have heard that Germany, Japan, the United States, all are working toward that type of technology, and there have been some impressive presentations about that. It really needs to be looked at, because if that were possible——

Senator BROWNBACK. That solves a lot of our problems.

Dr. HANSEN. It does solve a lot of our problems, but it is bound to increase the cost of coal use, so is China going to take that extra step to capture CO_2? They have a lot of coal.

So it is an open issue. I think it really needs to be looked at pretty hard.

Senator BROWNBACK. I just noted that in your testimony. That is very interesting. I was not familiar with how you would do that, but apparently that is being researched and looked at now. That is not known as a real solution.

I am sorry, I am going to have to slip on here, and I do not know that—I understand Senator Kerry is supposed to be coming back. Let me just say, if I could, in conclusion—and maybe he will come back in the interim here—is that a number of us are going to be working on ways that we can move forward on some no-regrets policies, items that have multiplicity of benefits you are talking about.

In addition to reducing CO_2, or in recapturing CO_2, there would be positive effects, and I think that in the state of play where we are as a nation and as policymakers at this point in time, that that is probably the best route to go, and I hear several of you suggesting that indeed is the route that you would suggest that we proceed. I hope you would engage us on a very open basis to suggest and to help us work through those so that we can start to address this issue that has been building for a long period of time that needs to be addressed.

There is still some cautiousness on some parts, but I think we can do things that at the end of the day we would say, there is no real reason why we should not do these steps.

I want to thank you all very much. We are going to stay in recess until Senator Kerry returns. If the panel does not mind for a few minutes we will be in recess.

[Recess.]

Senator BROWNBACK. I call the hearing back to order. Let me apologize to our panelists. I have been told that Senator Kerry will not be returning.

I do want to thank the panels and those that have been watching, and in attendance. I note there will be a subcommittee hearing on solutions, and these no-threat types of proposals, and we will be holding that within the next couple of weeks as we start to work through some plausible legislative solutions we can proceed with. The record will remain open for the requisite number of days for additional testimony to be submitted, or questions to be submitted. I thank the panelists again for being in attendance and sharing their views with us. The hearing is adjourned.

[Whereupon, at 11:30 a.m., the committee adjourned.]

APPENDIX

PREPARED STATEMENT OF HON. JOHN F. KERRY, U.S. SENATOR
FROM MASSACHUSSETTS

I want to thank Chairman McCain for holding today's hearing. As I have expressed to the Committee before, I believe that addressing the threat of climate change is one of the great challenges before the nation and the world. It certainly deserves the attention of this Committee.

Our topic today is the Intergovernmental Panel on Climate Change's Third Assessment Report. I want to take just a moment to discuss some of the history of the IPCC.

The Panel was created in 1988 to serve as an independent advisor to world leaders in assessing the scientific, technical and socio-economic information relevant for the understanding of the risk of human-induced climate change. Here in Washington that translated into studying the "scientific uncertainties" of global warming.

In an April 1989 appropriations letter to Congress, President Bush wrote, "Significant uncertainties remain about the magnitude, timing, and regional impacts of global climate change. During Fiscal Year 1988, the United States has made major contributions to international plans to reduce those uncertainties." Among the contributions the President noted was the Intergovernmental Panel on Climate Change, which, he said, "launched its multilateral effort in November 1988 with U.S. participation and support."

In a speech to the IPCC in February 1990, President Bush concluded that "human activities are changing the atmosphere in unexpected and unprecedented ways." And that, "the United States will continue its efforts to improve our understanding of climate change, to seek hard data, accurate models and new ways to improve the science and determine how best to meet these tremendous challenges."

I think the fundamental question before this Committee today is, "What have we learned in 10 years of study and three assessment reports from the IPCC?" My sense is the Panel has fulfilled its mission as an independent, scientific adviser to the nations of the world. It is also my sense that the Committee can place great confidence in the notion that human activities are contributing to rising atmospheric concentrations of greenhouse gases with potentially adverse consequences for the environment and millions of people.

Uncertainty exists—as it does in almost all matters of public policy—but that uncertainty has been reduced significantly over the past decade. And some uncertainty does not always justify inaction. In 1989, Secretary of State James Baker III spoke to the IPCC. He stated that, "[W]e can probably not afford to wait until all the uncertainties have been resolved before we do act. Time will not make this problem go away." I agree with Secretary Baker.

Unfortunately too many individuals, companies, nations and some in the Congress have used the fact that we can never be absolutely certain of how a natural system as complex as the global climate will respond to confuse the debate and undermine any meaningful policies.

That is why 10 years since Secretary Baker made that statement and despite more conclusive science, our nation has done so little to resolve the threat of climate change. Our emissions—despite our pledge to cut them in the Framework Convention on Climate Change have only grown. I hope Mr. Chairman, that this hearing will help build a foundation for the Congress to move constructively toward lowering our greenhouse gas emissions and responding to the threat of climate change.

In closing, Mr. Chairman, I want to express my disappointment in those who now attack the IPCC because they do not like its scientific conclusions. They assail the process of the IPCC and the motives of individuals who have lead the IPCC effort. Dr. Lindzen and my colleagues Senators Craig and Hagel have submitted such testimony today. I have listened carefully to their comments—and I respectfully disagree. I believe the scientists involved in the IPCC have done their best to provide an independent and honest assessment of the state of knowledge of the world's climate. It is an extraordinary charge we have given them, and I do not question their tremendous effort.

I thank the IPCC for its work. I thank our panelists for joining us today. And I thank the Chairman for holding this hearing.

RESPONSES TO WRITTEN QUESTIONS SUBMITTED BY HON. JOHN MCCAIN TO DR. VENKATACHALA RAMASWAMY

Question 1. The IPCC report states that climate models have evolved and improved significantly since the last assessment. However, the National Research Council reports indicates that US modeling capabilities trails those of Europe. Do you agree with that assessment?

I would like to first thank the Committee for the invitation to appear, and to present my testimony on climate change science. I am very appreciative of the thoughtful questions that have been put forward as follow-up to the testimony. In my testimony, as requested, I focussed exclusively on the scientific evaluations, following the details spelt out in the IPCC 2001 assessment. Partly because of the nature of the follow-up questions, I find that I have to go beyond the scope of the IPCC report, and include personal views in response to some of the questions.

Answer. On the first element under this question, coupled atmosphere-ocean climate models have evolved and improved significantly since the time of the previous IPCC assessment (IPCC, 1996). There is now improved knowledge of the physics based on theoretical and observational developments, including a longer observational record. For example, there is now an improved understanding of convection, radiation, boundary layer, and clouds, which constitute key climate feedback processes. These improvements have led to better representations of the physical processes in models and, therefore, increased credibility of the models to perform simulations of climate variations and change. There are now better simulations of climate, at least down to continental scales and over temporal scales from seasonal to decadal, including slight improvements in simulating El Niño. Confidence in model projections has also increased owing to the ability of climate models to maintain stable, multi-century simulations of climate; these are of sufficient quality for use in addressing climate change questions. Confidence in the ability of models to project future climates has been enhanced by the ability of several models to reproduce the warming trends in the 20th century surface temperature when driven by the known natural and anthropogenic forcings. Systematic intercomparisons of coupled climate models developed in recent years provides another line of evidence for the growing capabilities of such tools. Although there remain key uncertainties and quantitative aspects of key climate processes have yet to become robust, important scientific strides have been made in coupled atmosphere-ocean modeling since the last assessment.

The second part of the question touches upon a somewhat different issue viz., "US versus Europe's modeling capabilities". There are several sub-texts to be considered here. The first point is that there is no need to look upon the situation as a "US versus Europe" competition of an unhealthy type. It is more useful to consider our European counterparts as worthy collaborators in our joint quest to advance the knowledge in climate science. The investigation of climate and climate change is a massive scientific problem, and requires vast amounts of resources of various kinds in a globe-wide context, more than any one country could possibly support. To address this complex science, it is important to pursue the investigations in a cooperative and collaborative sense, recognizing that scientists in Europe (and elsewhere) may have as much and/or unique contributions to make to the advancements. It is in fact the recognition of this complexity and the need for a collaborative spirit that has led to IPCC's successful evaluations of the climate science, guided strictly by scientific bases and peer-reviewed publications. It is, however, incumbent upon US scientists to bear in mind always the highest traditions of science, and pursue the truth in an independent and original manner without biases.

Secondly, compared to Europe, and seen in purely computational facility and human brainware terms, it has become evident that the UK's Hadley Center (under the UK Meteorological Office) made a very focussed effort and posted substantive accomplishments, more than any other center in the world, during the latter half of the 1990s decade. There is one metric in particular that illustrates this point. The Hadley Center model has performed stable climate simulation integrations in excess of thousand years without flux adjustments—no other model in the world has been able to perform such integrations without flux adjustments/ corrections at the atmosphere-ocean interface. However, this model has been the only European climate model that has eclipsed the US achievements. It is important to note that no other model from any of Europe's other climate science institutions can be said to be more advanced than those in the US, with regards to the metric cited above or, for that matter, other metrics of relevance for long-term climate change.

It is a matter of considerable concern (and indeed has been recognized to be so by the Academy report) that the computational ability of the US has suffered a serious setback in the past few years. While European institutions have not had to think of changing basic architectures of their computational systems and have been able to procure the fastest computers available, US institutions have found their ability hampered in the procurements of the fastest computers in the world. And, there have not been many competitive alternatives available in this regard to the US institutions. Besides decelerating the pace of scientific research in the US, this factor has also initiated uncertainties about potential future computing frameworks for climate modeling research.

It is unfortunate, too, that the brainpower (i.e. talented human resources) needed to tackle the climate science problem has also suffered in recent years in the US. While European institutions and Hadley Center in particular have been able to ensure that funding and institutional infrastructure continue to be favorable enough to attract young students and scientists, such that they have been able to readily recruit bright and talented youth emerging from the colleges, US has lagged severely in this respect. Hadley Center has not only recruited top-class youth but has also motivated them into focussed climate modeling exercises. The problems in the US include: lack of resources to motivate the top minds in the country to turn to and remain engaged in science, declining base funding which barely if at all keeps pace with inflation, and declining infrastructure resources with lack of steady commitments to maintain top-class climate centers.

The above elements, while very crucial, have to be juxtaposed with a third one that is at least equal in value to those stated above. This concerns the question of extraction of science from the climate model simulations and observations. Obviously, it is not just enough to have the best computer, infrastructure and human resources. A key question is how far has the science been actually advanced. Examination of computer model simulations, critically analyzing them in conjunction with observational data of various kinds, and making incisive and proper diagnostic interpretations are the hallmarks of success in scientific research. This element, together with the others above, constitutes, in my view, the definition of the term "modeling capabilities". In this regard, it is not at all clear that the US contributions, in terms of the peer-reviewed findings reported in journals or in the IPCC reports, are any less relevant in originality and substance than contributions from Europe, including those from the Hadley Center.

The Academy document, while rightly pointing out the limitations of computer hardware and brainware, has chosen to critique a somewhat narrower focus of the overall problem. It has not emphasized enough that scientific accomplishments and advancement of knowledge in long-term climate change require more than just hardware and brainware. In particular, it has paid less emphasis to how the US has fared in the third element mentioned above. While Hadley Center may have unquestionably led in the implementation of the most sophisticated physics and thus created the most stable climate model simulations to-date, US institutions doing research in climate change have likely been not far behind Hadley center in the overall diagnostic analyses of climate change—forcings, feedbacks and responses. Compared to other institutions in Europe, there is no question that the leading US climate change research centers have at least been on par, if not outshining them.

But, it is easy to become complacent. Thus, it is important that US take firm, proactive steps to ensure sustained advancements in computer power, assure itself of a continued stream of talent to engage in the science, spot infrastructure deficiencies and build up with steady commitments. In turn, it should be demanded that scientific research continue to provide an unbiased, well-grounded and critical appraisal of the understanding of climate change to policy makers.

Question 2. How many more scenarios were involved in this recent assessment report as compared to five years ago? Would the scenarios used 5 years ago result in the new predicted increases in sea level rise and global-average surface temperatures?

Answer. The IPCC 1996 climate change science assessment employed the IS92 suite of scenarios (6 in all), with the middle of the range being the oft-mentioned IS92a scenario. In the 2001 assessment, the calculations drew upon the IPCC Special Report on Emissions Scenarios (SRES), besides also comparing the results with those from the IS92a scenarios (see Figure 5, IPCC Summary for Policymakers). The SRES was a separate study from the Working Group I climate change science assessment. The SRES scenarios were drawn up based on a range of diverse assumptions concerning future demographics, population evolution, economic developments and technologies. While a few of these new scenarios are similar to the IS92 set, some of the newer scenarios differ markedly from the earlier ones employed by IPCC. There were about 40 scenarios used in IPCC 2001, with 4 main groups or families, and with 6 "marker" scenarios. As an example, the IS92a scenario projection for carbon dioxide concentrations in this century is roughly comparable to that for the A1B and A2 scenarios. The IS92 and the newer scenarios represent quite a diverse collection of projections. Nevertheless, it is emphasized that the projections should be considered as sensitivity illustrations that employ a wide range of assumptions for the purposes of obtaining insights into the plausible projections of future climate changes due to anthropogenic emissions.

IPCC has discussed the projections of plausible future climates in terms of a range that is a consequence of the variety in the scenario assumptions. In arriving at the range of future climate change, IPCC 2001 considered the IS92 scenarios as well. The projections discussed in the 2001 report yield a range that encompasses the results of the IS92 scenarios, with the overall range wider now than in IPCC 1996. The change in the range from IPCC 1996 is due in part to the several new emission scenarios considered. The examination of both the IS92 and the newer scenarios in the 2001 report achieves the intent of surveying the effects due to an array of assumptions about emissions of radiatively-active species. Thus, the IS92a scenario (BaU) results for global-mean temperature and sea-level changes are indeed accounted for in the range cited in the 2001 report.

An important technical difference between the older and newer scenarios is the assumption of cleaner technologies in SRES which leads to differing considerations of the relative amounts of the projected concentrations of greenhouse gases and aerosols. In particular, the aerosol concentrations are affected by an earlier invocation of cleaner technologies in this century. As aerosols are short-lived, their concentrations are affected right away. Thus, the sulfate aerosol forcing concentrations (which yield a cooling) are projected to fall faster in the newer scenarios than was the case in the IS92 (e.g., IS92a) scenario. Greenhouse gas concentrations (including CO_2) rise less rapidly than in IS92a for several, but not all, of the newer scenarios. An additional feature in the IPCC 2001 report was to use the scenarios in conjunction with different model climate sensitivities to approximately mimic the range in climate sensitivity that arises owing to uncertainties in the physical processes.

Taking into account the ranges provided by the assumptions leading to the greenhouse gases and sulfur emissions, and the range in climate sensitivity, the following results are cited by IPCC (2001). The presently (and the most recently) cited range for the global-mean surface temperature change projected in 2100 is 1.4 to 5.8 C; this is to be contrasted with the range of 1 to 3.5 C in IPCC (1996). The main reason for the upper end being greater and a wider range has to do with the lower sulfur emission projections in the present report relative to the IS92 scenarios. Lower sulfur emission means lesser importance of the role of cooling effect by aerosols relative to the long-lived greenhouse gases. The corresponding global sea-level rise in the 2001 report is 0.09 to 0.88 m. This is to be contrasted with 0.13 to 0.94 m in the earlier report. Despite a higher temperature projected at the upper end of the range, the sea-level projections are lower owing to improvements in models that now yield a smaller contribution from glacier and ice-sheet melts. It is reiterated that the scenarios used five years ago yield results that are within the range spelt out in the 2001 report.

Question 3. You have stated that a key aspect of climate change is that a greenhouse gas warming could be reversed only very slowly. Can you elaborate on that point and also comment on the value in sequestration in this process?

Answer. The major greenhouse gas being input into the atmosphere, CO_2, has a long residence time owing to its chemical inertness. Its sinks act quite slowly; in particular, mixing into the oceans is very slow. Thus, it is expected that it would take a long time (centuries) to draw down the CO_2 that has been emitted. Other greenhouse gases, which are less strong climate forcing agents compared to CO_2, can be just as long-lived. In a general sense, there are several important climate forcing gases, with lifetimes varying from ten to upwards of hundred years (e.g., methane, nitrous oxide, halocarbons, sulfur hexafluoride). With the CO_2 sinks tending to operate slowly, even if it were assumed that all emissions ceased at present, there would tend to be only a slow decrease in the atmospheric CO_2 concentration.

The long residence time factor implies that the radiative forcing due to the emitted CO_2 will act for a long period of time. In addition, there is another timescale that has to be taken into account. This concerns the delay in the thermal response of the oceans owing to the long time it takes for heat to be diffused into or out of the deep ocean. At present, the climate is not in equilibrium with the present atmospheric CO_2 implying that the complete impact of present-day CO_2 is yet to be fully realized. Thus, while atmospheric CO_2 is not in equilibrium with the present emissions, the climate is not in equilibrium with the present-day atmospheric concentrations. Thus, even if the atmospheric CO_2 concentration were to be stabilized at a particular value and at a particular time, the climate effects can be expected to be felt well after this point is reached e.g., continued sea-level rise. The longer this forcing element is there in the atmosphere, the further the delay in the recovery of the climate system. In view of the slow but long associated timescales, greenhouse gas warming can be reversed only very slowly. In this regard, the possibility of non-linear and irreversible climate changes owing to feedback mechanisms existing in the system cannot be overlooked.

Sequestration process, meaning a mechanism to draw down the CO_2 thus reducing its atmospheric composition, would presumably achieve the objective of lowering the quantum of this forcing agent in the atmosphere. This is a conceptually attractive idea and one that is engaging vigorous research attention. Thus far, however, the research has yet to be translated in robust quantitative and practical terms, including cost-effectiveness. Early results are somewhat tentative on the overall effectiveness and scaling with respect to natural sinks, especially on multi-decadal to multi-century time scales. Note that even if it were possible to sequester all future CO_2 emissions, climate would still continue to warm and sea-levels would continue to rise, as noted above, because of the slow climate response to the existing atmospheric concentrations. Nonetheless, there are some interesting ideas concerning sequestration under active investigation which may shed further insights into this problem in the near future.

Question 4. The report states that a special need is to increase the observational and research capabilities in many regions, particularly in developing countries. How is this need being addressed by the International community and how much will it cost?

Answer. I will confine my remarks here only to the principal shortcomings. A key point to note is that observational networks are on the decline. Long-term monitoring of climate variables—even the most common and obvious ones, such as surface temperature and precipitation, are not being done with the spatial distribution and frequency that is necessary to achieve a comprehensive documentation of regional climate variations and change. The problem exists to varying degrees in all parts of the world, but is especially acute in the developing countries. Lack of adequate and sustained funding, the high cost of initiating and maintaining reliably measuring equipment, are major issues. There are, however, other factors as well, such as the lack of an appreciation of the significance of long-term monitoring, which inhibits a sustained high-quality data collection. Further, data gathering tends to not be a high-visibility exercise. The worth of such routine measurements does not really show up till at least a decade's worth of data has been collected. By then, due attention to such important technical issues as instrument maintenance and consistency in program management usually tend to wane, resulting in the difficulty of compiling a reliable dataset. Insofar as developing countries are concerned, the problems include acquisition of state-of-the-art equipment, ability to sustain funds for maintenance, and quality control. A recurring problem is the lack of well-trained human-power. As is true even the developed world, the scientific challenge posed by climate change detection is unable to compete with the marketplace attraction of other professions. Very few scientists' careers have advanced solely as a consequence of painstaking data collection over a long period of time, a timescale that is also considerably longer than typical program management tenure and fiscal considerations. Thus, especially among young scientists worldwide, there is a lack of a motivation to undertake these routine but necessary observations. This holds true in both developed and developing countries.

Automation and advances in remote sensing, which would obviate the need for humans to attend to the observational tasks, are not yet in full gear in this field in the developing countries. Amidst the pessimism, however, it is important to point out that some observational activities have indeed flourished e.g., measurements of CO_2 at a few sites around the world for the past 3 decades and more. This effort is particularly exemplary and is worth emulating for other climate variables as well.

The situation with regards to modeling capabilities, and diagnostic analyses combining models and observations is not dissimilar from the tenor of the issues plaguing observational datasets, as noted above. The lack of talented minds applying themselves to science in general and to this scientific aspect in particular needs to be improved. There is a need to improve this situation especially in the developing countries, where the educational and scientific infrastructure are at times too weak to sustain a orderly, long-term research commitment. International research organizations are trying hard to remedy the situation, but are being strained by funding inadequacy and the need to keep pace with the growing complexity of the climate system.

Question 5. What would you say is most urgent in terms of future research needs?

Answer. It is useful to summarize here IPCC 2001 's statements on future research needs. These are an appropriate recognition of the needs in the present times, based on considerations stemming from the current assessment of climate change science. Note that IPCC itself does not make any recommendations on prioritization or funding plans, nor is it associated with or endorses any national/international programs.

First, systematic observations and reconstructions of past climates need to be sustained and improved wherever possible. Observations include those that are designed to understand the processes, as well as those that are specifically geared towards long-term monitoring of key climate variables. The elements include: arresting and reversing the decline of observational networks; sustaining and expanding the observational foundation of climate studies by providing accurate, long-term, highly reliable and consistent data, including implementation of strategies for integrated and well-coordinated global observations; enhancing development of reconstruction of past climate periods; improving observations of the spatial and temporal distributions of greenhouse gases and aerosols; sustaining measurements that monitor forcing agents and climate feedback processes; improvements in observations of the world's oceans including ocean thermal changes (this may prove to be an optimal item to measure the increasing heat content of the climate system).

Second, improvements in modelling and process studies are needed to improve the quantitative realism of the simulated climate system. These include: improved understanding of the physical and chemical mechanisms that lead to a forcing of climate change; understanding and characterizing the important unresolved processes, and physical and biogeochemical feedbacks in the climate system; improved methods to quantify uncertainties of climate projections and scenarios, including long-term ensemble simulations using complex but well-understood models; improving the integrated hierarchy of global and regional climate models, with a focus on the simulations of climate variability, regional climate changes and extreme events; linking more effectively models of the physical climate and the biogeochemical system, and in turn improving the coupling with other factors intrinsically associated with human activities.

There is a vital research element to be added to the above viz., an appropriate synthesis of the observations and model simulations leading to a scientifically, well-grounded picture of climate change and its causes. Rigorous diagnostic analyses of observations and model simulations are critically needed in unravelling the evolution of climate change. Lastly, in the sequence, it cannot be overemphasized enough that each successive piece of knowledge gained, whether in modeling, observations or diagnostic analyses, needs to be gainfully used to plan better observational strategies and to improve further upon the model simulations/projections of climate change.

It is vital that there be a balanced approach that weighs in both observations and modeling studies. In particular, the build-up of the infrastructure and funding plans must recognize this point. For instance, observations should guide the science of what forcings are operating, what are the feedbacks, how should we be modeling these, what are the results of the simulations, how robust are they, how do they compare with various climate parameters, why is there a disagreement or why is there a good agreement, what can we relay back to the observational infrastructure so that they can receive better guidance. The idea should be to continually enhance the confidence in the climate forcings, feedback mechanisms, and responses, consistent with the central focus of understanding climate variations and changes.

Question 6. You have mentioned that the best agreement between observations and model simulations over the past 140 years is found when both human-related and natural climate-change agents are included in the simulations. Why is it important for the model simulation to include both?

Answer. In order to investigate the long-term climate change, model simulations of climate change have considered four different possibilities: (a) unforced internal variability of the nonlinear coupled atmosphere-ocean system i.e., the climate variations that occur even in the absence of any forcing; (b) climate change due to the introduction of "natural" factors such as solar irradiance changes and volcano-induced enhancement of stratospheric aerosol concentrations; (c) climate changes when only "anthropogenic" factors (e.g., emissions of greenhouse gases and aerosols) are considered; and (d) when all the factors are considered in unison. This modus operandi enables the identification of specific causal factors and aids in framing the detection-attribution analyses.

The climate model simulations performed indicate that it is very unlikely that internal variability of the climate system alone can explain the past 140 years' observed surface temperature record. Three different models (one of them from NOAA) are in agreement on this finding. The models' surface temperature interdecadal variation is not inconsistent with that observed over the past 140 years. A model simulation without consideration of the water vapor feedback yields far less variability than evidenced in the observations, suggesting that the manner in which this feedback is represented in the models may be qualitatively consistent with reality. Owing to the lack of a long record in atmospheric observations, there tends to be a reliance on climate models for estimates of the unforced climate variability. Although this is a limitation, there are tests that climate models have successfully met in this regard.

"Natural" factors alone cannot account for the observed warming over the past 140 years, although there are suggestions that over the first half of the 20th century, these factors may have contributed to the warming occurring at that time. In particular, solar irradiance changes may have contributed to the observed warming during the first half of the 20th century. Although episodic volcanic eruptions exert impacts during the 1–2 years that they enhance stratospheric aerosol concentrations, their effects over the past century are less relative to those due to the secular changes in greenhouse gases. Model simulations with "anthropogenic" factors alone indicate that, despite uncertainties in the quantitative estimates of the forcing, their influence in the model simulations can be associated with the rapid rise in the observed warming over the latter half of the 20th century.

When considering the entire modern instrumental surface temperature record, it becomes clear that both "natural" and "anthropogenic" factors need to be considered for the simulation of the observed temperature record. This includes the Sun's output changes as well as the particularly active volcanic period in the 1880–1920 and 1960–1991 time periods. For a proper explanation of climate change, and to distinguish between the natural factors and anthropogenic species, these factors must be juxtaposed with the internally generated variability.

RESPONSE TO WRITTEN QUESTIONS SUBMITTED BY HON. JOHN MCCAIN
TO JAMES J. MCCARTHY

Question 1. Why would climate changes in the 21st century be 2–10 times faster than those of the 19th century?

Answer. On pp. 30–31 of the oral testimony transcript I am correctly quoted as having made a statement like this in comparing rates of climate change between the 21st century and the 20th (not the 19th) century.

More specifically, this comparison is between the rates of global mean temperature change. For the 20th century this rate was 0.6C (1.0F) per century. For the 21st century, the scenarios project a range of increases between 1.4C (2.5F) and 5.8C (10F). This comparison is the root of the 2–10 fold comparisons.

Question 2. Your written testimony states that even the most optimistic scenarios for mitigating future climate change are unlikely to prevent significant damage from occurring. What type of events would qualify as significant damage?

Answer. Extrapolating from the changes that have occurred in the last few decades in the distributions and timing of seasonal biological phenomena, accelerating some of these by 2–10 times in the current century may push some species over the edge. Prime examples are tropical and Arctic systems, where temperature limits for some species like coral may be exceeded, and the ice habitat for many organisms, like pregnant polar bears needing the high fat nourishment of seals, may be lost.

Most problematic, though, are the impacts on human systems related to extreme climate events. Table 1 in the Working Group I SPM indicates levels of confidence in extreme weather and climate observations over the past 50 years and projections in the next 50 years. Table 1 in the Working Group II SPM lists representative examples of projected impacts from these extreme events. Extrapolating from the tolls in lives, livelihoods, and properties caused by the flood and mudslide disasters in the past 5–10 years to the projected future provides good examples of likely significant damage.

Question 3. There has been and continues to be a major discussion on how to reduce emissions. How can we best prepare people and systems for the disruption that will ensue with the climate change that is now projected for the 21st century?

Answer. This is in my estimation one of the most critical questions that we face. The scenarios mentioned above that yield the range of 1.4–5.8C increases are representatives of classes of scenarios (35 were used) that have several variable components. These include the projections for human population numbers over the next century, our standard of living and socioeconomic conditions in the developed and developing world, and the fossil-fuel intensity of our energy producing activities. The last of these is the one that is most easily altered with minimal impact on the other conditions.

While an optimist will suggest that it is unlikely that we will climb steeply up the highest of these slopes, a realist will also suggest that it is unlikely that we be able to stay close to the lowest of these slopes. Partly this is due to the socio-economic and geophysical inertia in our energy systems. While it is easier to modulate the use of fossil fuel, and especially to switch to alternative sources of energy, than it is to reduce the world's human population numbers, the difficulties in changing human behavior and human institutions are enormous. At the same time, since CO_2 emitted today will be still be in the atmosphere a century from now, everything we do now to reduce rates of emission will pay increasing dividends in the future.

This having been said, it is clear that we must also prepare for the sort of increasing prospect of damage mentioned in #2 above by enhancing adaptation. This is particularly critical in the regions hardest hit where adaptive capacity is the least (tropics and subtropics). Serious attention must be given to the potential impacts on the availability of safe water, subsistence agriculture, and human health.

How the scenarios mentioned above play out will greatly influence the rate of sea level rise. A large component of sea level rise is due to the expansion of the ocean as it warms. The convection of heat from the surface ocean to deeper waters is a slow process. A greater rate of atmospheric warming early in this century followed by a slower rate of warming later in the century will have a stronger effect on sea level rise within the next 100 years than a slow warming followed by a fast warming that would have atmospheric temperature at the same point 100 years from now. Coastal zones and small island states are vulnerable to this aspect of climate change and even more so with increases in peak storm wind and precipitation intensities. Planning for coastal human settlements, their infrastructures, and resources (like ground water) must be prepared to consider adaptive strategies that can minimize these impacts. Indigenous communities may in some instances be especially vulnerable, such as in the case mentioned for Alaska by Senator Stevens.

Question 4. Can you discuss some of the impacts of climate change on public health?

Answer. Impacts of potential climate change on human health are given a full chapter in the Working Group II report, and this is summarized in section 3.5 of the SPM. Broad categories include negative consequences of increasing thermal stress, the impacts of storms, and increases in the areal extent or seasonal duration of certain infectious diseases. In some areas there may be positive aspects of climate change for human health, such as with diminished winter mortality, but it is important to emphasize that the negative aspects will disproportionately hit the tropical and subtropical regions. An obvious adaptive strategy would be to enhance public health institutions and resources. Since these are woefully inadequate in many areas today, successful adaptation will take a concerted effort the likes of which is without any obvious precedent.

Question 5. How significant was last summer('s) passage of a ship through the Northwest Passage without touching ice? Has shipping traffic increased?

Answer. There is something symbolic and sobering about this observation. Had it occurred any time before in the last 150–200 years it would have been evident in the accounts of sealing and exploring vessels. It is possible that the thinning and loss of areal extent of summer ice in the Arctic Ocean and adjacent regions may be the result of a long term natural cycle, but the period of such a cycle must be longer than a few hundred years, and no known or hypothesized mechanism has this potential. Climate models have forecast diminished Arctic summer ice with continued greenhouse gas—forced warming, but the rates were less than has been observed in the last few years.

At this moment there are probably many commercial enterprises that are exploring options for capitalizing on the diminished ice in the Northwest Passage. Canadian claims regarding access through its Arctic archipelago are certainly an issue that that will require careful consideration by nations wishing to anticipate increased shipping potential through the Northwest Passage.

Question 6. You have mentioned how some species are being driven from their natural habitats because of changing environmental conditions due to increasing temperatures. How many species have been declared extinct because of these weather patterns changes?

Answer. As I stated in my testimony, it is not clear that any of the changes in distribution of species and the timing of biological processes (that can be plausibly liked to local climate change) have led to the loss of any species. Habitat destruction and the intentional and accidental introduction of invasive species have caused several extinctions, especially on islands. These may continue to be larger factors than climate change with regard to extinctions, but in the Arctic and the tropical ocean this condition may not hold—climate change may dominate. There are synergistic interactions among some of these factors, such as climate change prompting relocation of species, which is then hindered by land-use change that has interrupted migration corridors.

RESPONSE TO WRITTEN QUESTIONS SUBMITTED BY HON. JOHN MCCAIN TO DR. JAMES E. HANSEN

Question 1a. You mentioned that your alternative scenario assumes that air pollution is not allowed to get any worse than it is today and that global use of fossil fuels will continue at about today's rate. It also assumes no net growth of the other forcings. What are those other forcings?
Answer. They are included in Figure 2 of my submitted testimony. Chief among them are methane, tropospheric ozone and black carbon (soot) aerosols.

Question 1b. Does the IPCC business as usual scenario assume that air pollution is stable?
Answer. No, They have ozone and methane increasing substantially. In addition, they grossly underestimate the climate forcing by black carbon, and thus their scenarios tend to ignore it. Since air pollution is excluded from the Kyoto Protocol, it receives little attention in the IPCC scenarios.

Question 1c. Do these differences in assumption account for the differences in expected temperature increases in the next 50 years for the two scenarios? And again what are the temperature differences?
Answer. As shown in Figure 5 of my submitted testimony the additional warming in the next 50 years is about 1.6C in the business-as-usual scenario and about 0.75C in our alternative scenario. Moreover, the business-as-usual scenario "builds in" a much larger later warming, which will appear in the latter half of the century.
The smaller warming in the alternative scenario is due to the two assumptions: (1) it will be possible to stop further growth of non-CO_2 forcings (loosely labeled "air pollution"), particularly ozone, black carbon and methane, (2) it will be possible to keep the growth of atmospheric CO_2 to about 75 parts per million in the next 50 years, which would require that CO_2 emissions remain roughly similar to today's rate or decline slightly.

Question 2. You mentioned in your statement that the judge of science is observations. You also mentioned the potential educational value of keeping an annual public scorecard of measured changes. Can you elaborate on this idea?
Answer. It is briefly elaborated upon in reference 22 of my submitted testimony, where I mention an annual public scorecard of (1) fossil fuel CO_2 emissions, (2) atmospheric CO_2 amount, (3) human made climate forcing, (4) global temperature. I will try to write a paper with a more a more comprehensive discussion in the near future. One obvious addition would be an annual measure of CH_4 emissions and atmospheric amounts. However, the single most important benchmark for the United States is probably an annual update of the bar graph in Figure 11 of my testimony. i.e., the annual growth of CO_2 emissions the annual growth needs to be reduced to zero or slightly negative.

Question 3. Do you feel that your results were reviewed and properly considered as part of the IPCC process?
Answer. No. IPCC's size and review procedures make it inherently lethargic, so responding to a mid-2000 paper is difficult. However, the real problem is probably the close binding between IPCC and the Kyoto Protocol discussions. Kyoto excludes consideration of air pollution (such as tropospheric ozone and black carbon), for example, so IPCC basically ignores these topics and downgrades them. The only IPCC "review" of our paper was by the IPCC leaders (as reported in the New York Times, for example), who saw our paper as potentially harmful to Kyoto discussions. They received the backing of organizations (such as the Union of Concerned Scientists, who commissioned a criticism of our paper that I respond to in reference 22) and publications (particularly Nature), who had previous editorial positions favoring the Kyoto Protocol. When I had difficulty publishing a response in Nature, I wrote an open letter that is available at http://naturalscience.com/ns/letters/ns—let25.html.

Question 4. You mentioned that the climate cannot respond immediately to a forcing because of the long time needed to warm the oceans. How would we measure the real impact of reducing the amount of greenhouse gases in the atmosphere in the short term?
Answer. We should of course measure the individual greenhouse gases as the best measure of short-term effectiveness of any attempts to reduce emissions. However, the best measure of the impact of the net climate forcing is likely to be heat storage in the ocean. Natural variations of this rate will occur because of the dynamics of

the system. but if the measurements are accurate and maintained for years they will soon begin to provide us with a great tool for understanding where the future climate is heading.

A BRIGHTER FUTURE—BY DR. JAMES E. HANSEN

Contrary to Wuebbles' thesis (2002), most of the media did not misunderstand the thrust of our recent paper (Hansen et al., 2000). We do indeed assert that a scenario is feasible in which the rate of global warming declines. We also posit that, with an understanding of the significant climate forcings, it is possible to achieve such a climatically brighter path with actions that are not "economically wrenching", indeed, actions that make economic sense independent of global warming.

Our paper does not denigrate the "business-as-usual" (BAU) scenario that has been popular in global climate model simulations. The BAU scenario provides a valuable warning of potential climate change if the world follows a path with climate forcings growing more and more rapidly. Our aim was to present a companion scenario that stimulates discussion of actions that help avoid a gloom and doom scenario. I tried to clarify our objectives in an "Open Letter", which is made available from *Climatic Change* I summarize here key points of discussion.

Black Carbon (BC). One of our assertions is that BC (soot) plays a greater role in climate change than has been appreciated. We believe that the forcing due to BC is of the order of 1 W/m^2, rather than of the order of 0.1 W/m^2, as assumed by IPCC (1996).

My present estimate for global climate forcings caused by BC is: (1) 0.4±0.2 W/m^2 direct effect, (2) 03±015 W/m^2 semi-direct effect (reduction of low-level clouds due to BC heating; Hansen et al., 1997), (3) 0.1±0.05 W/m^2 "dirty clouds" due to BC droplet nuclei, (4) 0.2±0.01 W/m^2 snow and ice darkening due to BC deposition. These estimates will be discussed in a paper in preparation. The uncertainty estimates are subjective. The net BC forcing implied is 1±0.3 W/m^2.

Air Pollution. Aerosols and tropospheric ozone (O_3) are not addressed by the Kyoto protocol. They should be. A reason proffered for excluding ozone is that its chemistry is so complex that "most scientists" eyes glaze over" (Revkin, 2000). Perhaps the latter assertion is true. But it is not adequate reason to exclude air pollution from international climate negotiations. Our estimated anthropogenic global climate forcing due to BC (1 W/m^2) and O_3 (0.4 W/m^2) is comparable to the CO_2 forcing (1.4 W/m^2). One thesis in our paper is that halting the growth of air pollution can make a significant contribution to slowing global warming.

Effects of air pollution on humans are large in the developed world and staggering in the developing world. A recent study (Kunzli et al., 2000) estimates that particulate air pollution in France, Austria and Switzerland takes 40,000 lives annually with health costs equal to 1.6% of the gross national products. An example for the developing world is the estimate (Smith, 2000) that 270,000 Indian children under 5 years old die annually from acute respiratory infections caused by air pollution. Most of the pollution in this latter case arises from indoor combustion for cooking and heating, a primary source of the cloud of pollutants now mushrooming from India and China. Aerosols and ozone also reduce agricultural productivity with costs of many billions of dollars.

Practical benefits of air pollution reduction accrue immediately, not in 100 years. We assert in our paper that this offers an opportunity to reduce the climate problem with a cooperative approach that has immediate clear benefits to both developing and developed countries.

Methane. We conclude that climate forcing by CH_4 is 0.7 W/m^2, fully half as large as the forcing by CO_2. Observed growth of CH_4 is not accelerating, contrary to assumptions in many climate scenarios. Indeed, the growth rate has declined by two-thirds in the past 20 years. However, future trends are uncertain.

The task of understanding CH_4 should be jumped on, like a chicken on a June bug. Yet research support has been minuscule. We need quantitative understanding of CH_4 sources and sinks to define optimum policies. It may be possible to find practices that reduce methane emissions while saving money. Farmers want cows and beasts of burden to produce milk, meat, and power, not methane. Rice growers seek food and fiber, not methane, but we must also compare impacts of altered practices on N_2O production. There is much potential for methane capture via improved mining and waste management practices.

Scenarios. Science works via iterative comparison of theory and observations. Differences found are not a problem—on the contrary, only by discovering and investigating these can our understanding advance. One problem with the IPCC reports is that each report produces new (and more numerous) greenhouse gas scenarios with little attempt to discuss what went wrong with the previous ones. As a result, dramatic changes that have occurred since the 1980s in prospects for future climate forcings receive inadequate attention.

Figure 1 shows climate forcing scenarios used for climate simulations in the 1980s (Hansen et al., 1988). The actual climate forcing in 2000 is close to that of scenario B, and the derivative (growth rate) is less than that of scenario B. Further slowdown is needed to achieve the path of the "alternative scenario". The fact that the real world does not now *seem to be* following a path toward the median of the greenhouse gas amounts projected by Ramanathan et al. (1985) for 2030 in no way detracts from that paper, which, in my opinion, was one of the most stimulating papers in atmospheric sciences during recent decades. Indeed, to at least a small extent, one might credit the slowdown in climate forcing growth rates to the warning implicit in this and related papers.

Why have growth-rates fallen below BAU scenarios? One clear reason: the Montreal Protocol, which forced a phase-out of CFCs. That is an example of what we propose: actions useful for other reasons that also help to slow climate change. Reasons for the decline in the CH_4 growth rate need to be understood better. The apparent flattening of the CO_2 growth rate is probably due in part to an increased CO_2 sink, which may (or may not) be a temporary phenomenon.

CO_2 scenarios are the most critical. Our approach, characterized as naïve by Wuebbles, emphasizes observations. We note that the growth rate of CO_2 (fossil fuel) emissions has declined from about 4%/year to 1%/year in recent decades. It is noteworthy that the current IPCC (2001) scenarios have a growth rate in the 1990s that is almost double the observed rate of 0.8%/year (linear trend fit to 5-year running mean), but it is consistent with their failure to emphasize data. I will not characterize the IPCC approach defended by Wuebbles, but I note in my open letter the difficulty inherent in multiplying assumptions about population, economic development, and technology 50 or 100 years in the future. In my letter I specifically discuss their population estimates, which already appear to be unduly pessimistic.

Media and the Public. Wuebbles claims that the press misunderstood our paper. I believe that he fails to see the forest for the trees. The media do not always get technical details correct, as scientists know well. Moreover, media often have editorial positions and put their own spin on news stories. I complain in my open letter about an exceptional case in which *Nature* disguised their editorial position as a "news" article in which they report only criticisms of our paper. However, overall the media deserve credit for correctly conveying the thrust of our perspective on climate change. Indeed, the *Washington Post* editorial discussed in my open letter is, in my opinion, an astute assessment of the issues.

A basic problem is that we scientists have not informed the public well about the nature of research. There is no fixed "truth" delivered by some body of "experts". Doubt and uncertainty are the essential ingredient in science. They drive investigation and hypotheses, leading to predictions. Observations are the judge.

Sure, some things are known with higher confidence than others. Yet fundamental issues as well as details are continually questioned. The possibility of finding a new interpretation of data, which provides better insight into how something in nature works, is what makes science exciting. A new interpretation must satisfy all the data that the old theory fit, as well as make predictions that can be checked.

The suggestion that BC causes a forcing of about 1 W/m^2 is a possible example. Observations required to verify the forcing are extensive, because it is the sum of several effects. Perhaps recognition of the BC forcing will allow IPCC to include fully the negative direct and indirect forcings of sulfate and organic aerosols, something that they have been reluctant to do. There is still much to be learned.

In my letter I note the potential educational value of keeping an annual public scorecard of measured changes of (1) fossil fuel CO_2 emissions, (2) atmospheric CO_2 amount, (3) human-made climate forcing, and (4) global temperature. These are well-defined quantities with hypothesized relationships. It is possible to make the science understandable, and it may aid the discussions that will need to occur as years and decades pass. It may help us scientists too. I am curious, for example, whether the IPCC (1996) conclusion that fossil fuel CO_2 emissions must be cut by 80% to stabilize atmospheric CO_2 at 550 ppm will be supported by empirical data as it accumulates.

Strategic Considerations. Wuebbles states that our scenario can not be "used in any sense as a strategy, particularly given the inhomogeneities in the aerosol distribution and radiative forcing". We do not try to specify a detailed strategy for dealing with global warming (nor does Wuebbles or IPCC). However, we do present an outline of a strategy and argue that its elements are feasible.

It is impractical to stop CO_2 from increasing in the near term, as fossil fuels are the engine of the global economy. However, the decline of the growth rate of CO_2

emissions from 4 to 1%/year suggests that further reduction to constant emissions is feasible, especially since countries such as the United States have made only modest efforts at conservation. The potential economic and strategic gains from reduced energy imports themselves warrant the required efforts in energy conservation and development of alternative energy sources.

The other requirement in our alternative scenario is to stop the growth of non-CO_2 forcings, which means, primarily, air pollution and methane. The required actions make practical sense, but they will not happen automatically and defining the optimum approach requires research.

A strategic advantage of halting the growth of non-CO_2 forcings is that it will make it practical to stop the growth of climate forcings entirely, in the event that climate change approaches unacceptable levels. The rationale for that claim is that an ever-growing fraction of energy use is in the form of clean electrical energy distributed by electrical grids. If improved energy efficiency and non-fossil energy sources prove inadequate to slow climate change, we may choose to capture CO_2 at power plants for sequestration.

Global warming is a long-term problem. Strategies will need to be adjusted as we go along. However, it is important to start now with common sense economically sound steps that slow emissions of greenhouse gases, including CO_2, and air pollution. Early emphasis on air pollution has multiple immediate benefits, including the potential to unite interests of developed and developing countries. Barriers to energy efficiency need to be removed. Research and development of alternative energies should be supported, including a hard look at next generation nuclear power. Ultimately strategic decisions rest with the public and their representatives, but for that reason we need to make the science and alternative scenarios clearer.

Finally, an amusing thing about Wuebbles" criticism is the space devoted to noting that, even if there is some cancellation of global mean forcings by aerosols and gases, there may still be climate effects due to the geographical inhomogeneity of the net forcing. That's right. However, he fails to recognize that reduction of particulate air pollution will *reduce* this inhomogeneity, not increase it.

REFERENCES

Hansen, J., Fung, I., Lacis, A., Rind, D., Lebedeff, S., Ruedy, R., Russell, G., and Stone, P.: 1988, "Global Climate Changes as Forecast of Goddard Institute for Space Studies Three-Dimensional Model", *J. Geophys. Res.* 93, 9341–9364.

Hansen, J., Sato, M., and Ruedy, R.: 1997, "Radiative Forcing and Climate Response", *J. Geophys. Res.* 102, 831–6864.

Hansen, J., Sato,M., Ruedy, R., Lacis, A., and Oinas, V.: 2000, "GlobalWarming in the Twenty-First Century: An Alternative Scenario", *Proc. Nat. Acad. Sci.* 97, 9875–9880.

Intergovernmental Panel on Climate Change: 1996, in Houghton, J. T., Meira Filho, L. G., Callander, B. A., Harris, N., Kattenberg and Maskell, K. (eds.), *Climate Change 1995*, Cambridge University Press, p. 572.

Kunzli, N., Kaiser, R., Medina, S., Studnicka, M., Chanel, O., Filliger, P., Herry, M., Horak, F., Puybonnieux-Texier, V., Quenel, P., Schneider, J., Seethaler, R., Vergnaud, J. C., and Sommer, H.: 2000, "Public-Health Impact of Outdoor and Traffic-Related Air Pollution: A European Assessment", *The Lancet* 356, 795–801.

Ramanathan, V., Cicerone, R. J., Singh, H. B., and Kiehl, J. T.: 1985, "Trace Gas Trends and their Potential Role in Climate Change", *J. Geophys. Res.* 90, 5547–5566.

Revkin, A. C.: 2000, "Debate Rises over a Quick(er) Climate Fix", *New York Times*, October 3.

Smith, K. R.: 2000, "National Burden of Disease in India from Indoor Air Pollution", *Proc. Nat. Acad. Sci.* 97, 13286–13293.

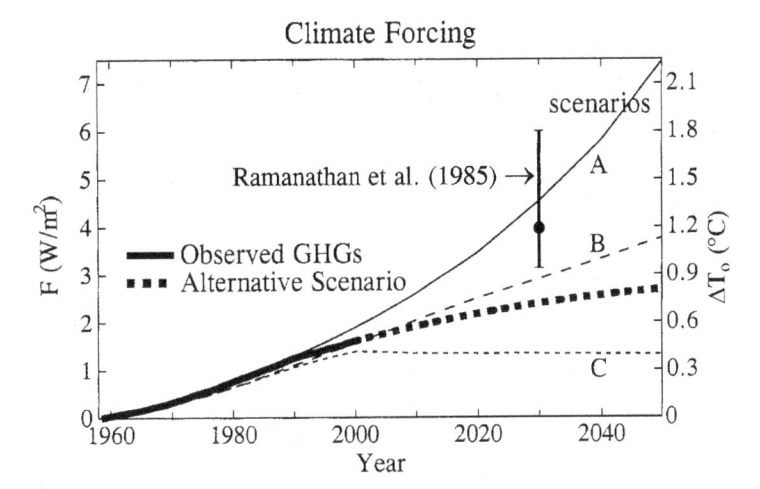

Figure 1. Greenhouse gas climate forcings for the scenarios A ("business as usual" or "fast growth"), B ("slow growth") and C ("no growth") of Hansen et al. (1988) and the "alternative scenario" of Hansen et al. (2000). Heavy solid curve shows actual climate forcing based on changes of CO_2, CH_4, N_2O, CFCs, stratospheric H_2O, and numerous trace gases. O_3 forcing is not included because of poor knowledge of changes and the expectation of partial cancellation between tropospheric increases and stratospheric decreases. Details are provided in a paper in preparation ("Climate forcings in the GISS SI2000 model"). The units for climate forcing employed by Hansen et al. (1988), $\Delta T_0(°C)$, the equilibrium global mean temperature change that would occur if there were no climate feedbacks, differ from the forcing in W/m^2 by the factor: $\Delta T_0(°C) \approx 0.3\ F(W/m^2)$.

[From The Washington Post, August 28, 2000]

HOT NEWS ON WARMING

If you're trying to decide whether to be an optimist or a pessimist on global warming, recent news is enough to leave you dizzy. An icebreaker found open water at the North Pole, prompting a new wave of attention to the thinning polar ice cap. That seemed like bad news, although some oceanographers said summertime cracks in Arctic ice aren't new, and this one shouldn't be over-interpreted. Texas, the state that produces the most greenhouse gas emissions, for the first time took steps to study the extent of those emissions and consider possible ways to reduce them. That was good news, although it doesn't guarantee state action. And Dr. James Hansen, a leader in drawing government attention to global warming, published a report suggesting that it may be "more practical to slow global warming than is sometimes assumed" by focusing in the short term on cutting heat-trapping gases other than carbon dioxide. That was surprising news, at least to those of us who have seen the climate-change fight centering on reducing carbon dioxide emissions.

It's long been known that carbon dioxide isn't the only gas that helps hold heat in the atmosphere. Six "greenhouse gases" were included in the Kyoto protocol, the international agreement that calls for cutting emissions by 2012. But carbon dioxide, the most abundant greenhouse gas, has dominated the public debate. It has been a subject of contention because it is a byproduct of burning fossil fuels, such as coal and gas, that drive modern industrial society. American opponents of the Kyoto protocol have argued that the reductions it requires could wreck the economy.

Dr. Hansen and a team of colleagues wrote that most of the global warming so far observed actually has come from other greenhouse gases such as methane, chlorofluorocarbons, and gases that combine to create ozone in smog. They suggested a strategy of focusing first on cutting those gases and black particles of soot that also trap heat. Some of the gases involved are already in decline because of other international restrictions; going after others amounts to an attack on air pollution, which the scientists argue should be attractive action in all parts of the world, independent of concerns about warming, because of the health benefits of cleaner air.

That optimistic scenario immediately caused some environmentalists to worry that the report would become a weapon for those who are skeptical about warming—who oppose any action. Dr. Hansen himself said it undoubtedly will be used that way, but that would be a misreading of the study. The new report does not challenge either the evidence that surface temperatures are going up or the growing consensus that human activities are contributing to the increase. It continues to cite the need for reductions in carbon dioxide emissions. There is no suggestion, nor should there be, that response to global warming should wait until the science is more certain.

What it does do is remind us that climate issues are complex, far from fully understood and open to a variety of approaches. It should serve as a caution to environmentalists so certain of their position that they're willing to advocate radical solutions, no matter what the economic cost. It suggests that the sensible course is to move ahead with a strong dose of realism and flexibility, focusing on approaches that are economically viable, that serve other useful purposes such as cutting dependence on foreign oil or improving public health, and that can help support international consensus for addressing climate change. If the Hansen report pushes the discussion in that direction, it will turn out to be good news indeed.

[From the International Herald Tribune, November 16, 2000]

TRY A COMMONSENSE RESPONSE TO GLOBAL WARMING

(By James Hansen)

NEW YORK.—Evidence continues to build that the world is slowly getting warmer. Almost all mountain glaciers are retreating. It was discovered this year that even the deep ocean is warming. On Earth's surface, where people live, the average warming is now about half a centigrade degree in the past 100 years.

Half a degree seems hardly noticeable. It is much less than weather fluctuations that occur every day. But it is a warning of possibly large climate changes as the 21st century progresses.

One worry is sea level, which will rise as glaciers melt and as ocean water expands from warming. A rise of a meter, a possibility this century, would submerge island nations such as the Maldives and the Marshall Islands, and it would be devastating to people living in Bangladesh and on the Nile Delta.

The greatest effect of global warming for most people may be an increase in extreme weather. Global warming is expected to cause more droughts and forest fires. It increases evaporation, which will lead, at other times and places, to heavier rainfall and floods.

The forces that drive global warming are no surprise. They are mainly the gases and fine particles that humans have been dumping into the atmosphere for many years. The gases, especially carbon dioxide and methane, absorb Earth's heat radiation and thus warm the surface, just as a blanket traps body heat. Fine particles of soot (black carbon) warm the air by absorbing sunlight.

Other human-made fine particles, especially sulfates, are nearly white. Sulfates come from sulfur in coal and oil, which is released to the atmosphere when these fossil fuels are burned. Sulfates cool Earth by reflecting sunlight back to space.

The net effect of these human emissions is not accurately known, because the fine particles are not yet measured well. But it is estimated that the net heating is at least one watt, perhaps closer to two watts, per square meter. Such a human forcing of climate is comparable to increasing the brightness of the sun by 1 percent.

Earth responds slowly to such forcings. The thermal inertia of the ocean delays the response. It takes decades for most of the response to occur, and centuries for the full response.

The question we face today is how much more we should allow human climate forcing to grow. That question is being addressed now in The Hague by the world's nations.

These deliberations are guided by climate simulations carried out by the Intergovernmental Panel on Climate Change. The simulations focus on a gloomy scenario in which it is assumed that humans will burn coal, oil and gas at faster and faster rates.

This gloomy scenario leads to an additional forcing of three watts in the next 50 years. Such a forcing will almost surely lead to increases in climate extremes and a rising sea level.

Some increase in human climate forcing is inevitable. Fossil fuels are our primary source of energy. Because of the energy infrastructure, it requires decades to phase in new technologies that may produce less carbon dioxide.

However, we recently suggested a scenario that reduces the human forcing to only one watt in the next 50 years. This would yield a more moderate climate change, allowing time to understand climate change better and develop technologies and strategies to deal with it.

There are two elements in this commonsense solution to global warming. First we must stop the growth of air pollution. This would eliminate any added climate forcing by constituents other than carbon dioxide. Second we must burn fossil fuels, and thus emit carbon dioxide, no faster than we do today. That means that growing energy needs must be met by increased efficiencies in current uses and by introducing technologies that produce little or no carbon dioxide.

Both elements are achievable but unlikely to happen by accident. Technologies that reduce air pollution have to be applied. Annual growth of carbon dioxide emissions, which has already slowed from 4 to 1 percent per year, must be slowed a bit further to zero growth or a small decrease.

Many actions could reduce both air pollution and carbon dioxide emissions. We need to develop clean fuels and renewable energy sources, and remove barriers to energy efficiency. Improved technology, perhaps including fuel cells and hydrogen power, can help reverse the trend to greater gas-guzzling vehicles. Utility profits should be designed to reward improved efficiency and decreased air pollution.

Improved energy efficiency, cleaner uses of fossil fuels and development of renewable energy sources will have multiple benefits. In addition to slowing the growth of carbon dioxide, this will create jobs, improve economic competitiveness, reduce reliance on foreign sources of energy and improve public health.

Fine particles in air pollution, including soot, sulfates and organic aerosols, penetrate human tissue deeply, causing respiratory and cardiac problems. A recent study found that air pollution in France, Austria and Switzerland alone accounts for 500,000 asthma attacks and 40,000 deaths per year. Air pollution in developing countries, such as India and China, is even more severe.

International cooperation is needed, because emissions circulate worldwide. But benefits of progress, in climate stabilization and health, will be similarly widespread. Required cooperation, including technology transfer, can include incentives and economic opportunities for all parties.

The commonsense approach is to move forward by attacking air pollution, improving energy efficiency and developing renewable energy sources. This approach is economically sound and has collateral benefits. It should provide a meeting ground for persons from a wide spectrum of political viewpoints, all of whom wish to preserve the environment.

RESPONSES TO WRITTEN QUESTIONS SUBMITTED BY HON. JOHN MCCAIN TO DR. RICHARD S. LINDZEN

Question 1. Your written statement refers to the limitations of computer models. In two recently released studies, computer models showed that the ocean warming that has been measured over the last half-century is exactly what would he expected from the amount greenhouse gases that have been emitted into the atmosphere. Tim Barnett of Scripps Institution of Oceanography is quoted as saying "This will make it much harder for naysayers to dismiss predictions from climate models." Would you comment on these recent reports?

Answer. The arguments in both papers are fundamentally circular as have been all attribution claims so far. What both papers show is that in response to rising surface temperatures of the past 50 years or so, there has been an increase in ocean heat content. Nothing controversial here. The emphasis of Levitus et al on the quantity of heat in the ocean is simply a statement that the heat capacity of the ocean is high; this is the reason for the ocean delay. Again no surprise. The claim that the observation confirms an anthropogenic cause is arrived at by looking at climate models which stimulate the observed surface temperature history by considering the joint effects of increasing C02 and aerosols. The argument goes that if models can stimulate the surface temperature, and if observations show then deep ocean heat content responds to surface temperature, then deep ocean heat content is responding to anthropogenic forcing. However, the aerosol forcing (which is crucial to stimulations) is so uncertain that it constitutes in essence an adjustable parameter (or parameters)which can be adjusted to produce a fit. The arguments of Levitus et al and Barnett et al then boil down to a peculiar assertion that if one can adust models to fit observations, the models must be right. Not exactly normative science.

That said, Barnett et al do mention some important things in passing. One was the role of the 'regime change' in the 1970's. This may be the real origin of temperature increase over the past 30+ years. The radiosonde data shows a very sharp increase in tropospheric temperature around 1976, with the surface temperature catching up over the following ten years (ocean delay again). This may be the reason for discrepancy between the satellite MSU data and surface data: the satellite data begins in 1979, after the atmospheric temperature rise occurred. As Barnett et al mention, the models don't show the regime change, and, therefore, the temperature rise they produce by adjusting aerosol forcing is likely due to the wrong reason. A second, was the comment that the coupled model they used was rather insensitive to anthropogenic forcing. This is important for the following reason: for sensitive models, the ratio of surface temperature to radiative forcing at the surface is high (this is the meaning of sensitivity), and low radiative forcing will cause the ocean to take longer to accumulate a given amount of heat. Relatively rapid heating of the deep ocean generally implies low climate sensitivity. In a paper by myself and Giannitsis in the Journal of Geophysical Research about 3 years ago, we looked at the observed response to volcanic sequences in order to estimate climate sensitivity: the range 0.3–1 .2C for a doubling of CO_2 appeared most likely (We are following the conventional practice of expressing sensitivity in terms of the response to doubling CO_2). More recently, at the meeting of European Geophysical Society a couple of weeks ago, we did the same for the surface response to regime change—and with the same result. Barnett et al really can't do the same since they don't know the actual forcing.

Which brings me to the final point: although both papers claim to have made an attribution (spuriously as far as I can tell), neither claims to have established any sensitivity, and it is the question of climate sensitivity that is crucial. Attribution without determining sensitivity is a fairly abstract exercise with no practical implication per se.

Finally, it should be pointed out that when these two papers compared observations with model outputs, the agreement was not particularly good.

Question 2. On the IPCC process, you have stated the vast majority of the participants played no role in preparing the summary, were not asked for agreement. Can you elaborate on this statement?

Answer. The IPCC directorate chooses the coordinating lead authors for each chapter. There were 13 chapters in the Working Group I report. Then a team about 15–30 lead authors are assembled for each chapter, and finally another 40–50 contributing authors are chosen for each chapter. (The numbers are approximate) Each 2–5 pages has about 2–3 lead authors responsible for their preparation with assistance from contributing authors. Only the lead authors, however, attend the meetings where their pages are prepared and reviewed. The meetings are held around the world. For Working Group I, the meetings were in Paris, Arusha in Tanzania, Auckland in New Zealand, and Victoria in British Columbia. Although each lead author may comment on the whole chapter, in practice, the lead authors generally concern themselves with the pages they are expert in. After the chapters are completed (in the case of Working Group I, this happened in August 2000), the coordinating lead authors prepare a draft of the Summary, which is then studied by the directorate as well as representatives from government, industry and NGOs who proceed to rewrite the summary. This was done in Shanghai in January 2001 for the Working Group I report. The resulting Summary for Policymakers is not subject to approval by any of the authors. Moreover, the directorate reserves the right to modify the chapters in order to make them consistent with the summary. This is done with the assistance of the coordinating lead authors. The text is not issued until months after the Policymakers Summary.

Question 3. You have mentioned that the preparation of the report was subject to pressure. You said that you personally witness co-authors being forced to use their green" credentials in defense of their statements. Can you explain these "green" credentials?

In the sections on water vapor of Chapter 7 (Physics of Climate), there were three lead authors (myself, Herve Letreut of France, and Ray Pierrehumbert from the University of Chicago). Although Letreut is a modeler and Pierrehumbert is a Sierra Club activist, and both wanted to stress that the models might be right with respect to the crucial water vapor feedback, we all agreed that the relevant physics should be briefly reviewed with errors from previous IPCC reports corrected, and that the potential problems be explained. When, the writeup failed to include the traditional bromides of the first and second assessments, the coordinating lead author, Thomas Stocker of Switzerland, who knew nothing about the water vapor feedback, insisted that the pages be rewritten to produce what was expected, and accused the three of us of being unduly influenced by my allegedly contrarian and suspect views. However, I had intentionally stayed out of the writing, and Herve and Ray were forced to explain that they were actively pro-environmental and supportive of global warming: they were only trying to tell the truth. The scene was truly pathetic, and was witnessed by others.

Question 4. Background: Last year I introduced a bill, titled "International Climate Change Science Commission Act", to established an International scientific commission to assess changes in global climate patterns and to conduct scientific studies and analysis for other nations. Given your experience with the IPCC, are you recommending that the US and other countries rely upon another scientific body such as the International commission that I proposed last year?

Answer. I am not familiar with your bill. However, I am not sure how the US would go about creating an international commission. Certainly, it might be possible to create such a commission without a tie to any negotiations, and a permanence that would be independent of 'crisis' and a charge that included understanding, monitoring, and eventual forecasting of climate change regardless of its cause.

Question 5. You have stated that if we view Kyoto as an insurance policy, it is a policy where the premium appears to exceed the potential damages, and where the coverage extends to only a small fraction of the potential damages. In your opinion, what type of damages would not be covered?

Answer. If one considers most warming scenarios, and carefully estimates the costs (viz Questions 2 from Sen. Kerry), they are at worst comparable to the estimated costs of Kyoto, while Kyoto will, at best, help us to avoid only a small fraction of the projected warming.

RESPONSE TO WRITTEN QUESTIONS SUBMITTED BY HON. JOHN KERRY
TO DR. RICHARD S. LINDZEN

Question 1. You have stated repeatedly and with some certainty that a doubling of carbon dioxide in the atmosphere will produce a warming of 1 degree Celsius at most. The IPCC has expressed far greater uncertainty in its estimate of the warming impact of a doubling of atmospheric carbon dioxide, offering a range of 1.5 to 5.8 degrees Celsius. On what do you base your conclusion and why do you make that conclusion with such confidence that you don 't suggest a range of warming?

Answer. In my written testimony, I mentioned that the response to double CO_2 alone, without feedbacks from clouds and water vapor, would produce about 1C warming. This is what virtually everyone involved gets. I also mentioned that higher values resulted from positive water vapor and cloud feedbacks in the models which have never been confirmed in the observations. Indeed the wide range of model results (which for a doubling of CO_2 remain in the range 1.5–4C which is what was given in the 1979 Charney Report of the NRC) results largely from the erratic behavior of clouds in the models. The IPCC range is based on the range of results produced by current models plus uncertainties in emissions scenarios with the highest value based on a scenario which more than doubles CO_2. In recent papers (including one in preparation), we have sought observational estimates of sensitivity and feedbacks, and have pretty much narrowed things to a range of 0.3 to 1.2C which represents (in percentage terms) as great an uncertainty as the IPCC model range of results. In a paper by myself and Constantine Giannitsis, we looked at the temporal response to volcanic eruptions which provides a direct measurement of sensitivity. In another paper by myself, Ming-Dah Chou, and Arthur Hou, we used data to estimate a negative cloud feedback completely absent from models which essentially cancels model positive feedback—even if the latter were correct, which seems unlikely.

Question 2. You argue that warming observed in recent decades "represents what is on the whole a beneficial pattern." You have also suggested that future warming may have beneficial impacts on the whole. What specific imnpacts do you view as beneficial and what impacts do you view as harmful in drawing that conclusion? What nations will benefit the most from warming? What nations will benefit the least or be harmed by warming?

Answer. With respect to my remark in the testimony, "that warming is likely to be concentrated in winters and at night . This is an empirical result based on data from the past century. It represents what is on the whole a beneficial pattern," the answer is fairly obvious: longer growing seasons, less frost, fewer cold related deaths, lower heating bills, less likelihood of older citizens moving to the moving to the sun-belt. In addition, there are the benefits from CO_2 fertilization: greater agricultural productivity with less need for water. The dangers are more speculative. Some endangered species may be stressed further, and some changes in preferred agricultural crops may be disadvantageous. Most scenarios of a catastrophic nature, refer to storminess, sea level rise, droughts, floods, etc., but these are even considered by the IPCC to be speculative since observational evidence is very weak, and in the case of extra tropical storminess, and variability, theory suggests the opposite (as noted in my written testimony). Finally, although I believe current models exaggerate the magnitude of warming. the coupling of these models to economic models with due concern for the detailed impact of climate change on specific sectors leads to a positive impact of GDP in most of the world. The figure is taken from a report by Prof. Robert Mendelsohri of Yale using Jim Hansen's model at the Goddard Institute for Space Studies. It shows most of the Northern Hemisphere benefitting, while parts of equatorial Africa and South Asia suffering reduced GDP.

FIGURE 3
GLOBAL ECONOMIC IMPACTS USING GISS

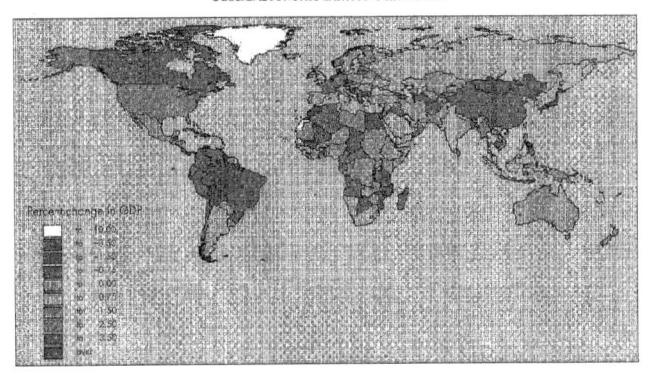